*Copyright © 2015 by Howard Spielman*
*All rights reserved*


*Illustrations © by Howard Spielman*


*Printed in the United States of America*
*First Printing: May 2015*

*ISBN-978-0-692-44163-3*

# A GOOD DAY

## Confessions of a Reformed Pessimist

By

Howard Spielman

*DEDICATION*

In loving memory of my mother, Harriet Moss Shapiro, who taught me that all things are possible for those who believe.

## ABOUT THE AUTHOR

Howard Spielman's varied careers span over three decades and have garnered him awards and accolades in every one, whether as an art teacher, writer, creator and executive producer of television shows, or fine artist.

With a bachelor of Fine Arts degree from Brooklyn College and a Master of Fine Arts degree from Pratt Institute Mr. Spielman began his working life as an art educator.

A partnership with his brother Ed Spielman (who was the creator of the original "Kung Fu" TV series), resulted in the creation of numerous TV shows. The most notable of these is "Dead Man's Gun" for Showtime. "Dead Man's Gun" received three Cable Ace Nominations, including "Best Dramatic Series", three consecutive Western Heritage Awards for best fictional television and was selected by the Orange County Register as "one of the top twelve series on the air."

Mr. Spielman and his wife now live in Florida. He divides his time between writing and creating Fine Art.

Howard Spielman's art may be seen at:

www.howardspielman.com

## ACKNOWLEDGEMENTS

I am blessed to have many good and expert people in my life who have also become friends. I would like to recognize the following people who helped to bring this book to fruition.

A huge thank you is due to my wonderful wife and story editor, Shirley Spielman, who painstakingly proofed and edited every word, line and page in this volume.

I am especially appreciative of Jim Mangano who, at a critical moment, brought home to me the power of choice in our lives and set the theme for this book.

Many thanks are also due to story editors, Deb and Ed Higgins and Pamela Hunt, who unselfishly gave of their time and expertise to polish these pages.

A big thank you is also due to Professor Ron Norvelle for his wonderful cover design. Missi Elmquist thoughtfully provided the photograph for the cover.

I greatly appreciate my friend and master problem solver Rich Jacoby.

Finally, I am enormously grateful to my brother Ed Spielman, the creator of the Kung Fu T.V. Series, who many years ago introduced me to the writers' craft and mentored me along the way.

# Table of Contents

Prologue: Half a Glass ............... 9

Fish Tales ................................. 12

Puppy Love ............................. 28

Bored of Ed ............................. 37

Don't Bug Me .......................... 49

Zeesa ...................................... 67

The Grass Is Always Greener .. 79

A Day At The Beach ................ 92

Hot Fudge ............................. 104

The Funeral .......................... 109

Car Trouble .......................... 117

Shark! ................................... 128

The Pond .............................. 140

The Man In The Green Suit . 161

V.I.P. .........................................177

Garage Sale ............................188

Moving Daze ..........................210

Dream House ........................229

Angel .....................................241

Family Ties ............................250

Ship Ahoy ..............................265

The Pelican Incident ..............289

# Prologue: Half a Glass

I had been a pessimist for a very long time. Not that I wanted to be one, but it just kind of happened in the course of daily living.

"Am I this way because I've experienced too many disappointments?" I wondered. I thought that perhaps I was pessimistic because I had been the victim of too many upsets. When you're upset much of the time, how can you avoid becoming pessimistic? Like all of us, I've been lied to on more than one occasion. Over the years I had been cheated by a fair number of people as well. I certainly had been cut off on the highway more times than I could count. And what about the government and the politicians? Was it any wonder that I had a pessimistic outlook on life? The surprising thing to me, given the nature of things, was that there were any optimists left in the world at all.

I once had lunch with a friend and she later confided to me that, after listening to my pessimistic views on a variety of subjects, she was depressed for the rest of the day. That was kind of a wakeup call. Not wishing to become a pariah in the community and have people begin to avoid me, I embarked on a mission to become a more positive, more optimistic person.

I bought self-help books by the car load which really didn't help all that much, except possibly to enrich the authors. Maybe I just wasn't ready to receive their messages. I even took classes to discover how to become more optimistic. The results were mixed. For the longest time I concluded that I came by my pessimism honestly.

So naturally when I learned that there was yet another new course being offered entitled "The Nature of Upsets," I immediately signed up. It was given over a single day and what I learned was very surprising. It was shown that, for the most part, upsets are not necessarily the result of bad things happening, but rather are often a product of our unfulfilled expectations. This was quite a revelation to me. I suddenly realized that my life had been going along rather well but not necessarily in the direction that I expected. The instructor of the course explained, and it was demonstrated, that the reason most of us are upset so much of the time is we just don't always get what we expect.

Well, if that's true, then how does one avoid being continuously upset and ultimately developing a pessimistic outlook? The possible answer is to embrace what you do get. Whatever happens might even be better than what you expected in the first place. Anyway, you are going to get what you get, so you might as well accept it.

My maternal grandmother, an exceedingly wise woman, had an expression that she tended to use on almost all occasions. It was only after taking the course on "upsets" that I realized how profound and all encompassing her often used comment actually had been. Whatever was happening at the time, she would neatly sum things up by saying, "Well, that's what it is!" Now who could argue with that?

This is not to say that we shouldn't plan our lives and strive to achieve our goals. But when our expectations are temporarily unfulfilled, we need to understand that being upset will not change the result one little bit. Rather, we should channel that disappointment into planning and striving again. I arrived at this personal realization after many unfulfilled expectations and much lost energy.

In this volume I will share with you true experiences that happened to me over the course of many years. While they were upsetting in varying degrees at the time, looking back I've concluded that, fortunately, they were not, with one exception, overly tragic. Thankfully none were fatal. They were merely experiences. Each can be likened to the classic example of the half filled glass.

The optimist says the glass is half full. The pessimist insists that the glass is half empty. Clearly they are both right. Both are simply viewing the glass from opposite perspectives. The following are some of my more memorable unfulfilled expectations. As you consider each glass in turn, I invite you to judge. Are they half full or half empty?

# Fish Tales

## *City Kid*

I grew up in Brooklyn, New York, in what I remember as a magical time and place. The apartment building where our family lived was essentially a vertical neighborhood where everyone knew everybody else. On warm days elderly women, including my grandmother, sat outside on beach chairs solving the world's problems while supervising the younger children.

Our park was the vacant lot down the street. During those early years whenever my mother asked my brother and me where we were going our answer invariably was, "To the lot, Ma." No jungle gyms, no swing sets, just an acre of dirt and pebbles with a sprinkling of broken glass for flavor. What better playground could a city kid ask for?

For us kids there were certain seasons that came and went, each in their special turn. We had a season for marbles when we all first learned how to gamble. I remember losing my favorite shooter at the lot to a dead-eyed kid who knocked it out of a circle we had drawn in the dirt.

The gambling escalated to a serious level during baseball season when we flipped baseball cards and matched heads or tails to see who won. The cards came with flat sheets of bubble gum inside the package as if the pictures of major league players were not enough incentive for young boys to buy them. Considering the number of cards that I accumulated and the amount of gum that I chewed, it's surprising that today I have any teeth at all.

Years later, as an adult, I walked into a comic book and baseball card store. The owner of the shop was wearing a tee shirt with a message printed on it. It read, "I own this store because my mother didn't throw out my baseball cards."

He was one of the lucky ones, I was not. My mother, rest her soul, always insisted on a clean house and years later in a burst of spring cleaning zeal disposed of my entire baseball card collection and my chance for early retirement. But to give Mom her due no one realized at the time when I was busy flipping original Brooklyn Dodger cards against the wall of our apartment building that one day collectors would be clamoring for each and every one of them.

There was also a season for cap pistols that fired paper caps that had just enough gunpowder or the equivalent in them to make a pop when the toy gun was fired. I can remember the trauma at age six of running out of caps during a serious game of Cowboys and Indians and being shot down by the other kids who had the foresight to bring more ammunition to our gunfight than I did.

When pea shooter season arrived, the kids in our building went to war with the enemy children that occupied the apartment house around the corner. A pea shooter for those unfamiliar with this particular weapon was an oversized plastic soda straw that fired either whole or split dried peas. It worked sort of like an Aborigine's blowgun, hopefully without the lethal result. The potential for damaging one's eyesight, however, was a genuine risk during the pea shooter wars, but it was one that six and seven year old boys were more than willing to take.

A surreal but much sought after visitor to our block was "POP, THE PEANUT MAN", as he was known. I say surreal because none of us kids ever saw him arrive and no one ever saw him leave. All of a sudden Pop seemed to just appear standing there next to his push cart. Pop had built the cart himself. It consisted of a flat shallow wooden tray about five feet square divided into many small compartments. The tray rested on two huge wooden wheels that he had also constructed by hand. Pop's creation was probably the sole surviving example of pushcart construction in the whole city because I never saw another one like it. Upon seeing Pop, all of us kids raced into the building to beg our mothers for a nickel.

Each one of the compartments of Pop's pushcart held tempting treats neatly packaged in small glassine bags. There were pistachios, walnuts, pecans, cashews and every other kind of nut you could imagine. There were chocolate candies and sugary treats of all descriptions plus jelly beans and much, much, more. The contents of the cart may have been a Dentist's nightmare but they certainly were a child's delight. Probably more for an interest in making a profit than for any concern about our dental health, Pop had placed only a very small amount of nuts or confections in each glassine bag. We dealt with this lack of quantity by eating our newly purchased treats as slowly as possible in order to make them last.

We always asked Pop, "How much?" for the particular bag that we had chosen. The answer never varied because, unlike the merchants of today, Pop's prices never changed. Each bag was always a nickel, but we asked anyway.

Once our purchases had been made we turned our attention to our snacks and each other. Some of us ate every morsel of what we had bought while others traded part of their candy in order to get more variety. By the time we looked up, Pop was gone. We never saw him push the heavy cart away. He had simply and suddenly vanished as he always did, not to be seen again until he magically made his next appearance.

The older boys played endless games of stickball in the street. Miraculously, no one ever was run over. Using a broom handle as an improvised bat, a heavy hitter could swat a pink rubber ball at least "two sewers", the distance measured between two manhole covers.

We younger kids naturally were forbidden to play in the street so we had to content ourselves with stoop ball. The object of this game was to throw a rubber ball against the steps of the apartment building and try to catch it before it hit the ground. Should the ball go into the street, the game was delayed until an older boy or adult retrieved it for us.

Oh, it was a great time to be a kid.

## *The Carp*

My grandmother lived in another building directly across the street from us. Once, when I was visiting, she went next door to speak to a neighbor and I went with her. As we entered the small apartment I noticed that the bathroom door was open and the tub was full. Strangely, there was something moving under the surface of the water. I looked over the edge of the bathtub and was shocked to see a large fish swimming slowly back and forth. It was a carp about two feet long. Of course I had seen small tropical fish in pet shops, but I had never been this close to such a big fish before. I sat there mesmerized as it swam rhythmically around the tub. I even touched it gently as it passed beneath my fingers.

"Wow," I thought, "this was great. Imagine, having a giant fish in your very own bathtub!"

As a little kid, it never occurred to me to question where the neighbor had gotten such a prize or even why she had a fish in her bathtub in the first place. All I did ask was, "Can I come back tomorrow and see the fish?" My Grandmother's friend told me that I was welcome to visit as often as I liked. So each of the following days I asked my mother to take me across the street to visit my grandmother. Mom was surprised and pleased that all of a sudden an active young boy like me wanted to spend so much time with an aging grandparent. I didn't think it was necessary to mention that the quality time I was really after was with a fish.

My mother patiently did as I asked for the whole of that week. On Sunday morning we made our daily trip across the street. Again my Grandmother shepherded me next door to the neighbor's apartment. Once inside I rushed to the bathtub to greet my new playmate.

Stunned, I stood there not fully accepting what I was seeing. The tub was completely empty. The fish was gone. But where? Not comprehending, I asked my Grandmother's neighbor, "What happened to your fish?"

Her answer was even more shocking to my immature sensibilities as I heard her say, "Oh, we ate it for supper."

"You ate him? How, how could you do that?" I stammered.

"Well, dear," she said, "that's why I kept him in the tub all week. You can't get a fresher fish dinner than the one we had last night."

I just couldn't believe it. I was horrified. They had eaten my fish. It hadn't been their pet at all, it was food.

The answer to how such a large fish got into the neighbor's bathtub is simple. Way back then the neighborhood fish markets had tanks of carp. This species has the ability to survive for quite a long time out of water. People would buy the live fish which would survive the trip home in a paper bag. They would then keep it active in their bathtub until its time was up. As a six-year-old, I knew nothing of this. Being a kid, I was inconsolable for at least an hour before childish distractions liberated me from the feelings of grief I was having over the loss of my finny friend. But I never forgot him, and this, my first serious unfulfilled expectation.

## *The Auction*

There was, however, a positive side effect from my early traumatic experience. It peaked my interest in all things fishy in general, and ultimately led me to a love of fishing in particular. But being a city kid with limited resources, the closest I could come in those early years to the wonders of the great outdoors was to eagerly read whatever magazines I could lay my hands on. With each monthly issue I tried to learn the proper bait, or lure, or technique to successfully land each species of fish in turn. From trout fishing in Iceland to salmon fishing in Alaska I devoured every article. Many years later the trout and salmon remain undisturbed as I've never been to either place, but I have hope.

There were many fishing tackle ads in the magazines. One company offered a five dollar surprise package of assorted fishing lures which my brother and I would beg my mother to send for on a regular basis. Even though in those days money was tight for our family, Mom would usually indulge us. When the package arrived the real surprise was if there was anything inside that was actually any good. Most of what we received was junk but as young kids we didn't know that or care. We couldn't wait to try out every swimming lure, fly or popping plug. Bursting with excitement we would tie my mother's sewing thread onto each of the lures and drag them back and forth in the bathtub for hours, imagining that we were fishing. It didn't matter a bit to us that the swimming plugs had difficulty swimming or that the popping plugs hardly popped at all. In our youthful imagination we were fishing and that, plus the occasional hook in a finger, was as close to an actual outdoor angling experience as we were likely to get for a while.

So, when I was about ten years old, I heard with great excitement my mother announce that she was taking us to the Catskill Mountains for the summer. Our destination was to be a bungalow colony in the heart of upstate New York. Today these unique summer communities have virtually vanished from the scene having given way to Caribbean vacations and cruises to far off places. But in those days they were very popular with urban dwellers of limited means who wanted to escape the brutal heat of New York City.

Bungalow colonies were privately owned and came in varying sizes. Some occupied large tracts of land while others consisted of only a few acres. The main house, where the owner lived, was usually surrounded by the bungalows rented out for the season. These were small one or two bedroom wooden cottages without any heat or insulation. None was needed as they were only occupied during the summer months. A three bedroom bungalow was a rarity and would have been considered palatial. A tiny kitchen area often had only a two burner stove, a small refrigerator and sink. The living conditions were primitive but no matter. We were out of the city and in the country until school started again in the fall.

Our colony had a small pond on the property where my brother and I learned to fish in earnest. By this time I had acquired an actual fishing rod and reel. The quarries we sought for the most part were the legions of sunfish and perch that inhabited the pond and made up in numbers and flavor what they lacked in size.

The pond had a small spillway that handled the overflow water and created a shallow stream which meandered under the nearby road and on into the woods beyond. One day I decided to stand on the overpass and fish this clear flowing stream. It was really hot so I had no shirt on. All I was wearing was a pair of shorts and sneakers.

I leaned over the railing, which kept the unwary from falling the several feet down into the stream below, and dutifully cast my lure. I retrieved it time and again with no strikes to be had. I didn't care. I was doing what I loved to do best and that was fishing. My attention was suddenly drawn to an elderly gray haired woman walking down the road toward me. As she got closer to where I was standing I noticed that she was wearing her Sunday Best. Despite the summer heat she wore a very fancy long dress accented by shiny patent leather shoes and a matching patent leather purse. This seemed to me to be an odd outfit for a walk down a hot dusty country road but she appeared comfortable enough in her finery. She was no doubt coming from a neighboring Bungalow Colony and was out for an afternoon stroll.

She walked up to me and stopped.

"What are you doing, Sonny?" she asked.

I thought this a rather silly question considering that I was standing over a stream holding a fishing rod. But since I was taught to be polite to my elders I simply responded, "Fishing."

She leaned over the railing, stared at the flowing current for a moment, made a sour face and proclaimed, "The water looks dirty."

I didn't know what she was looking at, since the stream was two feet deep and clear as glass. You could see each and every colored pebble on the bottom. I suppose that the elderly woman just felt compelled to rate the activity that I was engaged in and decided to give it a negative rating. She probably had been handing out negative ratings her entire life. Unfortunately some people are just like that.

In the very next moment the water exploded as a large pickerel hit my lure. This fish looks like a small fresh water barracuda and pound for pound puts up an equivalent battle. It is also very good to eat. I had fun reeling it in and brought it up and over the railing.

As I was unhooking my catch the old woman asked, "Sonny, what are you going to do with that fish?"

"I'm throwing it back."

"I'll give you a nickel for it."

Isn't it interesting the way a person's perspective changes as the situation does? Just a moment before, this lady who had decided that I was fishing in a polluted environment now wanted to buy a fish taken from the very same water.

"I thought you said the water was dirty," I not so politely observed.

Completely ignoring my comment she repeated, "I'll give you a nickel for your fish."

"Forget it," I told her as I held it over the railing in preparation for its release.

"Wait!" she shouted. "A dime. I'll give you a dime for it."

"No way," I insisted. "You'll have to do better than that."

So, standing over that stream at the tender age of ten, I held an impromptu fish auction. As I continued to pretend that I was going to release my catch, nickel by nickel, the purchase price went up. Finally, we agreed on the princely sum of twenty five cents for the freshest fish this old woman was ever likely to buy.

Sometimes I just don't know about people. After handing over the quarter she asked, "Sonny, do you have a bag to put the fish in?"

There I was dressed only in shorts and sneakers and this woman really expected me to produce a paper bag.

"No, I don't," I said. My manners forgotten, I just couldn't resist adding, "This isn't a fish market, Lady."

The old woman then reached into her purse and brought out a single crumpled facial tissue. She gingerly wrapped it around her slimy new purchase which she held stiffly out away from her body. I suppose she didn't want to mess up her fancy dress.

The last I saw of her she was kind of waddling down the road with her patent leather purse outstretched in one hand as she tried to balance the still struggling fish she stiffly held out in the other. I watched until she disappeared from view headed for the fish dinner of her life.

## *The Bass*

Our first season at the Bungalow Colony was such a hit with the family that we made it our regular summer vacation for several years thereafter. When I was old enough, and the pond and stream could offer no new challenges to my growing angling proficiency, my mother allowed me to explore the fishing opportunities available in the surrounding countryside. There was a medium sized lake not far away that I had been itching to try. Other fishermen had told me that it contained some huge largemouth bass. I was really excited about the possibility of landing one of the ultimate prizes of fresh water fishing.

Early one morning I got my rod, reel and my new tackle box and set out for the lake. Once I got there I was pleased to find that I was the sole fisherman at what looked like an ideal spot on a perfect sunny morning. There was a small beach that gently sloped into the water. The lake was glass smooth, with many patches of lily pads, and just enough open water in front of the little beach for me to cast my recently acquired collection of expensive bass lures. I had never caught a largemouth bass before, but in preparation for this day, I had read every article I could find on how one should go about the tricky task of besting this elusive quarry. I was armed with the right rod and reel, and I had carefully researched the subject. I was sure that I was ready. There wasn't a doubt in my mind that I would be successful. Oh, the best laid plans.

I had almost finished tying on a lure that a magazine article had promised would be a sure-fire bass killer, when out of the woods emerged another fisherman. He was an older man and dressed like a farmer. He wore denim overalls and a wide-brimmed straw hat. In one hand he carried a cane fishing pole about twelve feet long and in the other a large tin coffee can.

I was not thrilled to see another fisherman and my annoyance only grew as he proceeded to set himself up right in the middle of the small beach where I had planned to fish. In the process he never spoke a word to me or even looked my way.

This exceedingly rude fellow now occupying my spot was effectively blocking my ability to cast out to open water. If I tried a cast from any of the other available vantage points the many patches of lily pads would surely hang up my lure. As I was debating with myself whether to move farther down the lake the man started to bait his hook with the contents of the coffee can.

I took another look at the guy's fishing tackle. His twelve foot cane pole was made of a solid piece of bamboo, at the end of which was tied about another twelve feet of fishing line. The line on my reel was clear monofilament and designed so that a wary fish couldn't see it. This fellow's fishing line looked more like lightweight rope. When he was done fishing he could probably have hung his clothes on it. For all I knew maybe he did. I could cast a country mile with my fancy spinning rod and reel but this poor fool could only cover a twelve foot area.

His baiting technique was even worse than his old fashioned tackle. Night crawlers are the largest earthworms available and the man had a coffee can full of them. Normally these are ideal bait for bass if used correctly. All the fishing magazines said that the right way to entice a fish was to hook a single worm through the middle and let both ends dangle freely. With each end wriggling the fish should not be able to resist the bait. I had also read that it was preferable to use the smallest hook possible so as not to alert the wary largemouth.

This fellow had obviously not read any of the articles that I did because he threaded the first worm on a hook that looked more suitable for sharks than bass fishing.

This first worm was joined in turn by the rest of its fellows in the coffee can that were unceremoniously globbed on the hook until the whole mess looked like a big wormy meatball. There was not a dangling end to been seen. The final straw came when the man tied on a float about the size of a large grapefruit two feet above his hook.

I knew that a float, sometimes referred to as a bobber, was supposed to alert the fisherman when something was nibbling on his bait and offer no resistance should the fish decide to pull against the line. Considering the size of this man's float a great white shark might have difficulty pulling it under.

This guy clearly didn't know what he was doing. To my educated eye he obviously had no clue about how to catch a bass or anything else for that matter.

I wondered if maybe I should just wait a little while until he got tired of not catching anything and left. I was sure that I would get my spot back soon. I didn't know how right I was.

His foolish preparations complete, the man walked to the water's edge and whipped out his bait with all of his strength. The oversized float hit the water with a tremendous splash.

"Oh, great," I thought. "If there were any bass nearby this jerk just scared them into the next county." With only twelve feet of line tied to the end of his cane pole he could just as easily have flipped his bait gently out exactly the same distance without making hardly a ripple. It was clear that besides being a lousy fisherman this interloper was no rocket scientist either.

As the ripples radiated out from the float the man sat down on the beach and leaned back against a large rock. He pulled his straw hat down low over his face, folded his arms across his chest, and to all appearances prepared to take a nap.

Totally disgusted at this point, I gathered my stuff and decided to find a bozo-free spot to fish as far from this guy as I could get. As I was walking away I glanced back toward the lake.

"What a jerk," I thought. "All that guy's going to catch today is the nap he's after."

I had hardly taken more than a couple of steps when something on the water drew my attention. The man's ridiculously large float seemed to twitch just a little.

"It's probably just a passing breeze," I figured. "No fish is going to bite on that rig."

But there it was again. This time there was no mistake; the float was definitely twitching just slightly. To all appearances it looked like a school of minnows had located the worm meat ball and were delicately pecking away at it.

The man noticed it, too. With one boney finger he slowly pushed the brim of his hat up a little and studied his float which continued to twitch.

"Those minnows must be having a party," I decided.

As the float became more agitated the man pushed his hat further back on his head. It was only when the float very slowly began to move that he carefully picked up his rod. Since he had only twelve feet of fish line to work with the man held the cane pole out as far as he could over the water as the float traveled slowly away from the shore.

I stood there mesmerized not knowing exactly what I was watching. When the slack was almost gone from his line the oversized float suddenly disappeared with a loud "PLUNK."

The man leaned back on the cane pole with all of his strength and I watched awestruck as a giant largemouth bass came flying out of the lake like an unguided missile and sailed completely over the man's head. There was no fight, no playing the fish in a sportsmanlike manner. In fact, the guy had pulled back on the cane pole so hard that the fish never touched the water again at all.

The man quickly snatched up a large stone and raced to where the huge fish was flopping on the grassy bank. With one deft blow he quieted his catch by bashing it unceremoniously on the head. This guy had not a subtle bone in his body. He then picked up his cane pole and, carrying the immense fish, walked off into the woods without even a backward glance.

This entire scenario, start to finish, had taken place in all of five minutes. I was stunned. The guy had done everything wrong a fisherman could do and yet I had just watched him catch one of the biggest largemouth bass I had ever seen anywhere, including those pictured in the magazines.

I had to admit to more than a slight feeling of fishy jealousy.

I thought, "That should have been my fish. I was in the right spot at the right time. I had gotten here first. If I had just tied on my lure a little sooner I would have been the one to catch that monster."

After a long moment of self pity I decided that where there was one giant bass there had to be more. Besides, I was the one with the superior fishing tackle, not to mention the superior knowledge of the sport. If that dumb farmer could catch a bass then so could I. So I walked confidently to the water's edge and began to cast my brand new expensive killer bass lure. And I cast that lure over and over and over again all, I'm sorry to report, to no avail. I did get a chance to change lures when a wayward cast fouled my plug on a patch of lily pads and I had to break it off.

By the end of that morning I had tried every single lure in my tackle box with the same result. I had caught nothing except a newly acquired case of humility. But in retrospect maybe that wasn't such a bad thing. After all, a fish when served stays fresh for just a little while, but a serving of humility can last a lifetime.

# Puppy Love

It was the age of Rock and Roll and I was fourteen years old. On a whim I decided that I wanted to learn to play the guitar. Besides the fact that I was enamored of rock music, I'd heard that girls were rumored to like guitar players. I remembered a sign that I saw in the window of a storefront in the neighborhood advertising guitar lessons. The instructor and his wife lived above their music school. He didn't look like most people I was used to, with his shoulder length black hair and long fingernails that he expertly employed to play the Flamenco guitar. The man and his wife had just opened their school, were desperate for students, and eagerly signed me up for lessons. I agreed to rent an inexpensive guitar and purchased a book of sheet music. After each lesson I was told to go home and diligently practice.

I really wanted to be good at playing the guitar and faithfully did as instructed.

There was just a small problem though; I wasn't wired for sound. I believe that, with rare exceptions, most people have an aptitude for one thing or another, but not for everything. My mother was artistic and I had inherited her drawing skills; but music I simply didn't get no matter how hard I tried. So week after frustrating week I returned to the storefront and played for my guitar teacher. After each lesson I received a mandate to return home and practice even harder.

Two months of this went by and I had not progressed at all in my quest for musical mastery. After yet another frustrating lesson, my instructor turned to me and asked, "Is there anything else that you like to do?"

I thought that he was just making idle conversation as I answered, "I really like to draw and people say I'm pretty good."

"Well then," he said, "That's what I think you should be doing. The guitar is just not for you. You have no aptitude for it and, in my opinion, I don't think you will ever improve."

This totally took me by surprise. I knew my instructor really needed the money from the lessons he gave but he was kicking me out of his music school anyway. I remember having my feelings hurt at the time, but in retrospect the guitar teacher was truly a Man of Principle. Even in the midst of my great disappointment I knew he was right. I stunk at the guitar and realized that I would not be getting any better. He had done me a favor.

I returned to my first love which was drawing and forgot about my musical failure. I was reasonably content for a while until one day, at the high school, I saw her. I can't really explain what first attracted me. She wasn't that pretty. Actually, in all respects, she was basically quite average. But there must have been something about her because, from the moment that she turned in my direction, I was totally and hopelessly in love.

As an extremely unworldly high school freshman, having had zero experience with women, it was most certainly puppy love. But for me, at the time, I was sure it was the real thing. In fact, the feeling that I had for this girl was so strong it was almost painful. I fully understood the concept of Cupid's arrow because that's what I felt had just hit me.

In those days I was much, much too shy to approach her directly, so I made some discreet inquiries to find out her name, and learned that she was a cellist in the school orchestra. Instead of taking the direct approach as kids so easily do today and simply ask her for a date, I decided to hatch a plan to get close to the object of my infatuation. It was a different time and, as I said, I was painfully shy.

What to do? "I've got it," I thought. "If I join the band we'll be in the same class. We'll see each other every day. Once we're occupying the same piece of geography our relationship will naturally progress from there."

The fact that I had no musical ability whatsoever and would likely never acquire any did not deter me in the slightest. I was on a mission to win the object of my affections, and any musical limitations that I might have felt, I would just somehow have to overcome.

Congratulating myself on a brilliant scheme, the following day at school I marched into the music department and spoke with the chairman who also led the school orchestra.

"Can I help you?" he asked.

My immediate thought was, "You can help me get next to the girl of my dreams."

But I didn't say that. Instead I said, "Yes, sir, I'd like to play the guitar in the band."

"I'm sorry, Son, we have enough guitar players."

"All right, how about the drums?"

"I'm afraid not," he replied. "In fact, all the band instruments are taken."

"Well, what is available?"

"The only instruments that we have left are for the orchestra: the bass fiddle, the violin and the cello."

Oh, how stupid I suddenly felt. I had asked for a band instrument when the object of my affections played in the orchestra. The band and the orchestra practiced at different times in different rooms. Had I been given one of the band instruments I would never have even gotten a glimpse of her.

I weighed my options. Since every musician had to carry his instrument back and forth to school for practice sessions I immediately ruled out the bass fiddle as too heavy and cumbersome. Considering the violin for a moment I could see myself being accosted by the neighborhood toughs while carrying what most teenaged boys considered a sissy instrument. That left the cello. Actually that was perfect. She played the cello. I might even get a seat next to her. I couldn't believe my luck.

"O.K.," I said, "I'll take the cello."

The chairman of the music department signed me up and told me to report to the class the following day. That night I hardly slept as I anticipated seeing her at practice.

The students were setting up their instruments as I entered the basement music room. I eagerly scanned the faces but there was no sign of her. Well, it was early and I figured that she just hadn't arrived yet. The chairman noticed me and called me to his desk. He said that since the cello was new to me he would assign a student with more experience on that instrument to get me started. Wow, maybe it would be her! Would I get that lucky? How many cello players could there be anyway?

My joy was short lived as he summoned a thin girl with a sallow complexion and introduced me to my new cello instructor. My disappointment was easily matched by the girl's lack of enthusiasm for the additional burden in her life which was suddenly me. She grudgingly took me over to the cabinet where the instruments were stored and handed me a scarred and battered cello with a matching bow. I had never been this close to one before and to me it looked like a giant violin. But this thing you held between your knees and drew the bow across the strings as you pressed your fingers down to make the notes. Sounded easy enough I thought. She handed me a small block of what looked like plastic.

"What's this?" I asked.

"Rosin," she said. "You need to rub it on the bow so it won't slip as you play."

This was something I could handle. Under her watchful eye I rubbed the block of rosin back and forth across the bow strings. Satisfied that I had at least mastered the first step on my way to becoming an accomplished cellist she said that she had to get her own instrument and would return in a few minutes.

Trying to sound as casual as possible I asked her if she knew the girl I was really there to see.

"Oh, yes, of course. She's upstairs on the third floor with the main Orchestra."

"The third floor? Why?" was all I could manage to blurt out.

My new cello instructor explained that the Orchestra and the Band were organized by expertise and experience. My Girl, I had begun to think of her that way although we had as yet not even met, was very expert and played with the first Orchestra that performed the concerts for the school. The less experienced groups were levels two and three and practiced on the lower floors. My group, the least accomplished of all, wasn't even deserving enough to be assigned a number and practiced in this basement room possibly to avoid offending the ears of people passing in the halls.

The third floor! I had no idea that there were different Orchestra groups on different levels. How would I ever get close to her now? I decided that there was only one thing to do. I would just have to master the cello and work my way up, level by level and floor by floor, to the Promised Land.

The thin girl assigned as my teacher next showed me how to hold the instrument, how to place my fingers on the strings and demonstrated the proper way to draw the bow. I carefully did as instructed but my best efforts somehow produced vastly different sounds than the ones she made. In fact, if The Society for the Prevention of Cruelty to Animals had been located nearby, they would certainly have tried to find out who was strangling cats in the basement of the school.

My new instructor reminded me not to forget to rosin the bow. This last bit of advice I really took to heart. When the other students were busy tuning their instruments I was busy rosining my bow. When the others were arranging their sheet music I rosined my bow. Actually when the other students in the class were doing anything at all I rosined my bow. Since that was the only thing that l knew how to do, that was all I did.

I believe that my bow ended up with more rosin on it than any other cello bow in recorded musical history.

The next problem was the music book that I was given to practice with. I had never been taught to read music. The book was of no more use to me than if I had been handed a volume written in Sanskrit. I carefully omitted to inform the music Chairman of this minor detail, lest he eject me from the class and sabotage my planned ascension to the coveted third floor Orchestra.

The Chairman had us meet in small groups. We all had our varied instruments and our music books on metal stands. He called on one student at a time and each played the selection we were up to. Then the group turned to the next page and another student would be called on.

Some people swim mighty rivers for love. Others climb high mountains. But none endured more pain and suffering than I as I attended daily Orchestra practice in that dreary basement music room. I tried to fit in. I really tried. When the others turned the pages of their music books I blindly did the same. As my turn to play a selection became imminent I started to sweat and my heart began to race. Finally, when I was called on by the Chairman, I picked up my extremely well rosined bow without the slightest clue as how to actually create a single note of music. Before I had fully drawn it even a single time completely across the strings the Chairman held up his hand and said, "Good, good, that's enough."

It was obvious that my best efforts were an affront to his ears. I'm sure that I must have invented some brand new sounds that defied all classification. The Chairman was an accomplished musician in his own right but he worked in a public high school and was obligated to teach all who came before him no matter how inept they might be. The poor man was probably suffering almost as much listening to the strange noises emanating from my cello as I was producing them.

Two whole weeks of this musical torment for both of us passed before the music Chairman called me up to his desk. Public servant or not he could stand my presence in the group no longer. He sternly faced me and said, "You know, Son, not only do you have a tin ear but you're supremely tone deaf. Get out of my class."

I didn't know what a tin ear might be and I wasn't exactly sure what tone deaf meant, but I knew clearly that neither condition was acceptable for anyone attempting to ascend to the lofty heights of the third floor Orchestra. While I felt that the Chairman could have been gentler and more tactful in my dismissal from the class there was no arguing with the truth. I had to face the fact that, as a musician, I was a complete, total and absolute flop.

So, after leaving my budding musical career behind did I hatch another scheme to get close to my lady love? Did I formulate a plan B? Did we ever go out on a date? Did I even get up the courage to speak to her? The answer, I'm sorry to report, to all of these questions is a sad and pathetic, "No." In fact, she never even knew I was there.

In remembering this, my first childhood infatuation and an impossibly flawed scheme to get close to the girl of my dreams, it all seems so ridiculous now. It was purely and simply an adolescent delusion. But for me, somehow at the time it made perfect sense and I truly believed my plan would work. I've since learned that the youthful male brain is not fully developed until after the age of twenty. So I have to allow for the fact that mentally, way back then, I certainly was not hitting on all cylinders.

Although I may not have gotten the girl, the entire experience was not a total loss. I know that if I'm ever again called upon to rosin a cello bow, I'll certainly be ready.

# Bored of Ed

It was the time of the Vietnam War. I had just graduated from college with a degree in Fine Arts and a plan to become a world famous artist. What did I know; I was young. So imagine my shock when I opened the mail. I had heard about them but luckily had never seen one until that moment. I also never, ever dreamed that I would get one.

"Greetings," the letter began. As I read on, it fully dawned on me.

"Yikes, I'm drafted!"

At first I just couldn't wrap my mind around the idea that, instead of becoming a famous artist, I was going to be a soldier. War and the concept of kill or be killed was completely alien to my psyche. I just couldn't accept the idea. After all, I didn't even swat bugs in the house. I caught them in paper cups and released them outside unharmed. The more I looked at the official looking document the more real and scary my situation appeared.

I felt very sorry for myself. Here I was, all set to become a world famous artist and this had to happen. The government must have heard about my plans and deliberately stepped in to mess things up for me. With the stroke of a pen, someone at the draft board had arranged it so that I no longer had control over my own life.

"I don't even do so well in snowball fights," I thought. I was sure that if I got sent to Vietnam, I wouldn't be coming back in one piece. What to do?

The letter informed me that I had only two weeks before I needed to report for a physical. Not much time to figure something out. I had heard about people leaving the country and fleeing to Canada.

"Way too cold," I thought. "Besides, I'm an American and I wanted to stay one."

I just didn't want to be a soldier, or kill anybody and especially not get killed. Why didn't the government understand that I could serve my country much better by becoming a world famous artist?

Then Providence or something stepped in to change everything. My mother turned on the T.V. and saw a commercial. It was not shown a second time. It didn't have to be. The New York City Board of Education was advertising for teachers. It seemed that there was a shortage. The ad said that applicants with a college degree in any subject could take a ten week summer program to get a temporary teaching certificate. At the completion of the program they would be immediately employed by the city and be able to start teaching. The ad went on to say that by completing the program the applicants would be draft exempt.

I couldn't believe it. I was saved! Prospective draftees flocked in droves to sign up and avoid going to war. The city called the ten week crash course, "The Intensive Teacher Training Program," a.k.a. the "I.T.T.P." The idea was to make up the necessary education courses over several years after beginning your teaching career. Sounded like a plan to me.

There was just one thing though. I really, really didn't want to be a teacher. I wanted to be an artist. I vividly remembered sitting in my ninth grade art class watching some of my more rowdy friends torment our teacher unmercifully. She was a nice lady and didn't deserve the treatment those kids were dishing out. I remember at that time resolving never to become a teacher. And yet, here I was at this crossroads. Although I didn't want a career in education, I wasn't real keen on becoming a soldier either. I told my mom that I knew nothing about teaching and I had no interest in being a teacher.

She looked at me as if I had lost my mind and said, "You'll learn. At least no one will be shooting at you. Spit balls are a lot less painful than bullets. Now, go be a teacher!"

I couldn't argue with her logic. Face down in a rice paddy or teach. The choice didn't seem to be all that difficult. After a little more soul searching I decided to let the New York City Board of Education save my life. Besides, I figured, the war can't last forever. Maybe I could become a teacher first and a world famous artist later. Ah, youth.

I don't remember much about the ten week program except the heat. The course was given in a high school classroom that had no air conditioning. The room was filled with other draft evaders like myself with a sprinkling of female college graduates who had decided, for reasons of their own, to also become instant teachers.

Our instructor, an amiable down-to-earth sort, was a high school principal. He was full of practical advice for the fledgling educators seated before him.

He told us things like, "Be careful in the Teachers' Cafeteria. You might sit down at a chair that has been occupied by the same person at lunch for twenty years and unknowingly make an instant enemy."

"What does this have to do with teaching?" I wondered. "Oh well," I naively thought, "I'm sure we're learning just what we need to know to do the job."

On the final day of our ten week course we were congratulated by our instructor who issued certificates to the class and proclaimed that we were all now official teachers. He instructed us to report to the District Superintendent's Office for assignment to one of the Brooklyn high schools.

Funny, I didn't feel like a teacher. When I studied myself in the mirror I certainly didn't look like one. My sneakers, jeans and tee shirts were not the clothes of a teacher.

"Clothes! Yikes, I suddenly realized that I didn't have any teacher clothes! What do teachers look like anyway?"

I tried to remember. An image of my fifth grade teacher, a big woman in a flowered print dress suddenly popped into my head. "No, I don't think so."

My tenth grade Biology teacher flashed by my consciousness next. All I could remember about him was his shiny bald head, his huge walrus mustache, and the striped bow ties he was fond of wearing. Not the look I was after either.

My other big problem was money. I had very little of it. I decided that, at the very least, I needed a suit. I opted for a really cheap black one.

"Black goes with anything doesn't it?" I thought. I had forgotten about its incompatibility with chalk dust. So, my first foray into the world of teachers' fashions was what one of my future colleagues later uncharitably dubbed, "The Polyester Funeral Suit."

The District Office was located in a large elementary school. Entering the building were many I.T.T.P. graduates, as well as those dedicated souls who actually planned to become real teachers and had official degrees in Education.

We all signed in and were instructed to wait in the Student Library until we were called for our assignment. As we filed into the large room we looked for a place to sit.

I thought, "Is this a joke?" Since it was an elementary school, all the tables and chairs were scaled down to fit little kids. No seating accommodations had been provided for adults. After standing for an hour, several of us attempted to sit down in the Lilliputian chairs.

I wondered, "Is this a test to check if the I.T.T.P. people had good balance? Or could it be a subtle way to weed out the overweight people?"

Some of us failed the balance test and hit the floor but quickly regained our footing as well as our composure, and tried again. We sat on these diminutive foot stool sized chairs through most of the day. Well, almost all of us. Some of the more savvy new recruits were sent for never to return. I later found out that these more astute budding educators had the presence of mind to pre-interview at the more desirable schools and already had jobs nailed down. Their visit to the District Office had just been a formality.

"You could pick the school you wanted to work in and go there to interview for a job?" Nobody had told me I could do that. Actually, nobody had told me anything.

Finally, and it seemed like eons, my name was called. My body was numb from the waist down after several hours of sitting on a daycare sized chair. I was led to the office of the District Superintendent herself, a very heavy woman, with a pasty complexion and an impatient manner. On her desk was a large glass fish bowl full of slips of folded paper.

After glancing at my I.T.T.P. certificate to verify my eligibility to receive one of the coveted slips she reached into the bowl and retrieved one. Each school in the district had a number assigned to it for the purpose of a job lottery. My paper had the number three written on it.

"Go and see the secretary at the front desk and show her your number," the Superintendent commanded. "She'll tell you what school to report to."

I thought to ask a question like, "Is that it?" But by some electronic sleight of hand, the next applicant was summoned into the office and brushed past me to receive his number. I couldn't believe that the job of a District Superintendant included picking a number out of a bowl. There was no pretence of any kind of interview either.

Once at the secretary's desk I dutifully presented my number and was informed that I was very fortunate to be assigned one of the "better" high schools in Brooklyn. I later found out that an assignment to some of the other schools would have been more dangerous than actually going to war. She handed me a form letter of introduction and signed the Superintendent's name. I was told to report to my assignment at 8:30 am the following Monday.

I burst into the house and called to my mother, "Mom, I just got my assignment. They said it's a good school."

"That's wonderful, Dear."

"But what do I do, Mom? I don't know a thing about teaching."

My mother gave me that mother look and then applied mother logic.

"You just took a ten week course, you must have learned something."

"Ma, trust me, I didn't learn a thing except where not to sit in the Teachers' Cafeteria."

"It doesn't matter," she insisted. "You're not going to war and that's all that counts. The rest, you'll figure out as you go along."

Monday morning arrived all too soon. Armed with my letter of introduction I found myself standing on the sidewalk gazing up at an intimidating Gothic building that was supposed to be my place of employment for the foreseeable future. I stood there feeling very uncomfortable in my polyester teacher "Clo". I called it my "Clo" because other teachers had "clothes" but this one suit was all that I could afford. I glanced at my brand new Timex watch which had used up the balance of my meager funds. It read 8:20. I was ten minutes early.

"Remember," I told myself, "whatever happens in there they won't be shooting at you." So, mustering up my courage, I walked through the wrought iron gate and approached the front doors with trepidation.

"Well, here goes," I thought, and pulled the large metal handle. The door wouldn't budge. "It can't be locked!"

I tried the other one. But it was also shut tight as well. I checked the letter of introduction that I had gotten from the

Superintendent's Office and confirmed that I was at the right place. Another glance at my Timex verified again that I was here at the right time. So why were the doors locked?

I proceeded to circle the building like a cat burglar trying one door after another to no avail. Every single one was locked. Fighting to keep my growing sense of alarm from becoming full blown panic, I reviewed the possible reasons for my failure to gain access to the school building that I had been told to report to.

Reason One: Fate, Providence or Whatever had changed its mind and no longer wanted me to be a teacher. "See," Fate seemed to be saying. "How are you going to teach when you can't even get into the building?"

Possible Reason Two: I had the day wrong. Another likely indication that I was not cut out to be a teacher.

Reason Three: Unknown and yet to be determined.

Reason Three became increasingly clearer as my situation revealed itself. The educational system is severely flawed. One hand doesn't know what the other is doing. But I didn't realize this at the time. I thought that somehow, without knowing it, I had already messed up. Still, with visions of rice paddies again occupying my thoughts, I forged doggedly ahead. At what must have been the very last door of the school I pulled the handle and was vastly relieved as it opened with a satisfying click.

I entered the building and received another shock. The hallway was pitch black. No students or teachers or, for that matter, any signs of life at all were evident. I took a few tentative steps then had another moment of self doubt. I had almost turned to leave when I spotted a pin-point of light at the far end of the corridor. Like a moth to a flame, I turned toward it as a beacon of hope. My new cheap leather shoes pinched my feet as my footsteps echoed down the freshly waxed hallway.

As I neared the light I saw through a glass partition, a middle aged woman working at a desk in an inner office. She was illuminated by a goose neck lamp in front of her. Engrossed in her work, she did not hear my approach even when I got right up to where she was sitting.

I gently said, "Excuse me."

In the ghostly light of the single bulb the woman turned with a look of abject terror and saw me, a strange man in a black suit, standing over her desk in the darkened school building. She uttered a single, chilling high pitched scream as she levitated out of her chair and backed away. Startled, I jumped back also.

"What? What?" was all she could manage to gasp as she hyperventilated and clutched her chest.

"What? What?" was all I could manage at first as well, as I clutched my chest.

Both of us now quite shaken, I ventured, "I'm from the ITTP."

"What? What?" she repeated again, in a quivering voice.

Remembering my note, I took it out of my pocket and offered it to the terrified woman, who, it turned out, was the Assistant Principal of the school.

She took the note with shaking hands and read aloud, "This will introduce a graduate of the Intensive Teacher Training Program, who is assigned to your building." Signed, the Superintendent of Schools.

When the Assistant Principal finally managed to catch her breath and calm down a little she quickly dialed a phone on her desk. While I stood there I heard her say, "I have somebody here who says he's from the I.T.T.P. and that he's assigned to our school. No, I don't know what it is either. No, I don't know what to do with him either."

The Assistant Principal was speaking with the Principal of the school. Neither one of them had heard of the I.T.T.P. or me. Evidently none of the powers that be at the Board of Education had seen fit to inform the school administration of the existence of this supposedly vital program or of my assignment to the school.

Over the next few days they found menial work for me to do in various offices. This usually meant a day of filing since the students were not scheduled to arrive until the following week. It was apparent to these experienced educators that I was the furthest thing from a teacher they had ever seen. They were not about to entrust me with a class of my own even if they had one available for me, which they didn't. I was being paid as a teacher. I was exempt from the draft as a teacher. But everyone was clear, I was no teacher. I had to agree.

So when I reported for work the morning that the students arrived, I was surprised to find that I had actually been given an assignment to a classroom. It wasn't a teaching assignment. It was a senior homeroom class where all that was required was for the students to fill out attendance cards. My job was to hand out the cards, place them in alphabetical order, and put them in an attendance book. It sounded easy enough.

As I entered the classroom all the students stopped talking and turned my way. They seemed to be evaluating this interloper in their midst, and I felt that they could see right through me. Although they were nice kids I must admit to feeling very intimidated. Actually, I was terrified of these high school seniors. After all I was barely older than they were. Although I was really nervous I did manage to hand out and collect the attendance cards. Now to complete my assignment: put the cards in the attendance book. A simple enough task one would think.

The attendance cards were small thin pieces of cardboard. The book had cardboard pages as well with slots cut to receive each one. Since this was a new book the pages were stiff and you had to lift the edge of each slot with your fingernail in order to insert the cards. This tiny but crucial fact had been completely overlooked by our instructor during the ten week summer program. So, I just pushed the attendance card against the edge of the first slot and the card promptly bent in half. I pushed it again and the newly bent card simply jackknifed once more. Not sure what else to do I discarded that one and reached for the next. A second attempt to insert this card into the book met with the identical result. I began to sweat. After a half dozen tries I had six bent attendance cards scattered on the desk in front of me without having successfully inserted a single one.

They say the definition of insanity is to continually repeat the same action that gives you an unsuccessful result. By that measure I probably was a little crazy at the time. In my own defense, you have to remember that I was in that classroom feeling like a total fraud. No, let me amend that. I was a total fraud. Had I not been intimidated by the environment and the entire experience, and so scared of these senior kids, I like to think that I would have easily figured out what was required.

One of the senior boys seated directly in front my desk had been studying me the whole time as I futilely tried to insert each of the attendance cards in the book. Finally, he leaned forward and said, with a wolfish grin, "Don't worry, we won't eat you."

I'm not ashamed to admit, it was a tremendous relief to hear him say that.

And so… my teaching career began.

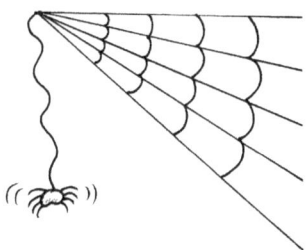

# Don't Bug Me

*Itsy Bitsy Spider*

Most people don't like bugs and my wife is no exception. But her primary fear in the entire world is spiders. She would prefer to go up against a great white shark or a grizzly bear with a butter knife rather than deal with even the smallest of that eight legged species. I'm not crazy about spiders either but her fear is off the charts.

One time a friend of hers invited us to a summer home on a small lake. It was to be a relaxing weekend getaway and we were both looking forward to it. We spent a pleasant day, enjoyed a nice dinner, and late in the evening were shown to our bedroom. As we were getting ready to turn in it began to rain really hard. It felt good to get into a soft cozy bed, pull up the comforter, and listen to the storm outside the window. The lake house was really old with antiquated lighting fixtures and exposed wooden ceiling rafters.

Our bedroom was illuminated by a single light bulb that was suspended from the cathedral ceiling by a long electric cord. The bulb was covered by a paper lampshade and hung down over the bed. I was just about to turn off the light when my wife noticed that, hanging by a single gossamer thread from the lampshade, was a spider no bigger than the head of a pin.

"Kill it," she demanded in fright. This is always her immediate and sole response to spiders of any size.

Without thinking, I gave it a back hand slap knocking it into the gloom of the bedroom. My wife got really upset then.

"I said to kill it not to swat it away," she said. "Now we don't know where it went to. I'll never be able to get to sleep worrying that it might creep on me in the night."

This time I felt that she was taking things too far. The tiny spider was so small that that I could barely see it. Even if it did crawl on us or even happen to bite us we wouldn't be able to feel it. She was completely overreacting to her arachnophobia.

"You'd better find it," she demanded.

"And just how am I supposed to locate a tiny thing like that in the dark?" I asked.

"I don't care how you do it. If you don't find, it I'm telling you, I can't stay in this room tonight," she announced with finality.

The lampshade was still moving from the slap that I had just given it and my attention was suddenly drawn to the attached electric cord swaying back and forth in the dim light of our bedroom. My eye followed the movement of the cord all the way to where it was connected to the high ceiling. It was only then that I noticed something very strange up in the darkened rafters. The entire ceiling seemed to be covered with a thick layer of cotton wool. The effect was almost like clouds that had somehow found their way indoors. But what was this? Covering the gauzy cloud material were many, many black spots of various sizes. They looked like black stars on a cloudy night.

Yikes! Was it my imagination or were the black stars slowly moving? I don't know why it took so long for it to register on my consciousness just what I had been looking at. Maybe because I had never seen or heard of anything like this inside a house before, but all of a sudden, to my horror I knew: they were spiders! And the cloudy material was a thick layer of spider web.

Looking at the largest of the black dots and considering how high the ceiling was I calculated that some of the spiders had to be huge. Here my wife was worried about one tiny eight legged critter getting away when right over our bed was a real live spider horror show. I knew that if she became aware of what I had just discovered, my wife would be in real danger of developing a sudden cardiac problem. As for me, there was no possible way I was going to get a wink of sleep under that giant web on the ceiling.

So I turned to her and said, "You know, I've been thinking. You're absolutely right. I'll never be able to find that little spider. I don't want to stay in this room tonight either."

There were no other guest rooms available for us in the house that night so we put on our clothes and made our way out through the rain to our car. If there is ever an award given to loving, patient and long suffering husbands, then I should get at least two for that cramped, damp and miserable night I spent trapped in a car with an unhappy wife. I stoically listened to her berate me for being an incompetent spider killer who had forced us to spend the long dreary night in our car. Through it all I never breathed a word of what I had witnessed crawling across that bedroom ceiling.

How had such a chamber of horrors as that guest bedroom come to be? The house belonged to the elderly mother of my wife's friend. We found out later that the old woman used it only infrequently and our particular guest room was seldom occupied. It probably had not been cleaned in years. This information my wife found out from her friend days later once we were safely at home. I was back in my wife's good graces once she became aware of the fate that I had saved her from.

## *Godzilla*

Several years passed and our aversion to lake houses had faded. So one summer, my brother, myself and our wives, decided to rent a place in New Hampshire for a week. The house had lake rights and access to a row boat. My sister-in-law's brother, a professor of Biology, was also going to join us. All of us were excited about an idyllic vacation in the country. We had been in the house just one night and part of a day and were really enjoying ourselves. The women prepared a nice lunch and we all sat down at the table ready to eat. It was then that my wife looked up and screamed. We all jumped out of our seats and turned to where she was pointing. There, right over the dining room table, was the biggest, hairiest spider any of us had ever seen. It was easily the size of my outstretched hand and was casually walking upside down across the ceiling.

Turning to me, my wife voiced that familiar female battle cry, "Kill it!"

She received my also familiar male response at moments like these, "Not me!"

My sister-in-law then turned to my brother and demanded, "You kill it!"

"No way! I'm not going near that monster," responded the other mighty hunter in the group.

My wife declared, "If neither of you brave men are going to kill the spider then I'm not staying in this house another minute!" And off she went to pack her things. My sister-in-law echoed the same sentiments and disappeared to pack as well.

All my brother and I could do was watch helplessly as this Godzilla of the spider world continued its slow march across the ceiling. It had taken over our vacation house and we were too paralyzed with fear to stop it.

I stood there contemplating the various consequences of our lack of bravery. The girls were packing to leave. The lakeside house had not been cheap to rent and there was not going to be any refund given for our early departure. Our vacation was about to be ruined and we were standing by powerless to prevent it. All of this was due to our cowardice in the face of a single, but admittedly very large, Arachnid. I shuddered to think of what life with my wife was going to be like once we got home. I was certain that I would never hear the end of this misadventure.

I've frequently said, "It's better to be lucky than smart." In what followed next, a variation that surely applies would be, "It's better to be lucky than brave." And did we ever get lucky. As if on cue, my sister-in-law's brother arrived just as we were fleeing the house.

"What's going on?" he asked. "Where are you all going?"

We explained the dire straits that we found ourselves in, spider-wise. He smiled and said, "Show me what you're all talking about."

We cautiously led the way back inside with the women bringing up the rear. The eight legged Godzilla was still slowly marching across the dining room ceiling without a care in the world.

Our visitor excitedly exclaimed, "Oh, wow! Keep it in sight and don't let it get away. I'll be right back. I have to get some things from my car."

And with that he was gone. I thought I could handle the keeping the creature in sight part but I hadn't a clue as to how I was supposed to stop the largest spider that I had ever seen from getting away if that's what it decided to do. Fortunately, our visitor returned in only a few minutes. In one hand he held a glass jar; in the other he grasped a butterfly net.

Now who travels with a butterfly net? Lucky for us this professor of Biology was never without his "catching net" as he called it. I watched in wonder as he unscrewed the jar which we later found out was filled with alcohol. He bravely stood up on the dining room table and approached the fearsome invader. With one deft swoop he whisked Godzilla into the butterfly net as we all drew back in abject terror. "Now he's gone and made the thing mad," I thought. But before I could turn to run, in the next second he had plunked the hairy creature into the jar of alcohol and safely screwed the lid closed.

All of us couldn't believe our eyes. Our visiting savior held up the jar and examined his captive in the same way a wine connoisseur would study a glass of vintage Cabernet. He broke out in a big smile as he pronounced the long scientific name for his prize.

He told us that Godzilla was a wolf spider, meaning that it didn't build a web but made its living just prowling around looking for a meal.

"It's a kind of tarantula," he said. "They're common around lakes in this area. This one is an especially large example of the species."

Our benefactor turned to us and said, "Thanks. What a perfect specimen. I don't have one of these in my collection."

"Thanks?" I thought. "He's thanking us? We were all leaving. If he had gotten here one minute later the house would have been deserted. And to think, he has a collection of those things." Our vacation was saved.

## *The Great Outdoors*

With her fear of insects in general, and being especially terrified of spiders in particular, it was a total surprise to me when, a year or two later, my wife announced, "I want to go on a camping vacation."

"You mean sleep on the ground in the woods?" I asked.

"No," she said. "On Madison Avenue. Of course the woods. What do you think?"

"Well," I gently inquired, "I thought that you had an aversion to bugs. The last I heard the Great Outdoors is a very good place to find them."

"Don't worry about it," she said. "I want to try camping. I used to love my Girl Scout summer camp." And that was it.

My idea of a vacation was more along the lines of going someplace that had a pool, room service and a soft bed, but I've learned that once my wife makes up her steel trap mind there is no point in trying to change it. Since we didn't have any equipment for camping we decided to rent what we needed.

Not knowing any better at the time we ended up renting a very large and excessively heavy army surplus canvas tent. We continued to prepare for our first venture in outdoor living by acquiring slightly less equipment and provisions than would be required for a trip up the Amazon River.

The morning of our departure I packed as much of our camping equipment as I could into our car. My wife came out of the house to inspect my progress and was not thrilled to see so many things still sitting there on the driveway.

"It doesn't fit," I told her. "We've got too much stuff."

"It'll fit," she said. "You just did it all wrong. Take everything out. I'll repack the car."

Not wanting to begin our trip with an argument, I grudgingly unpacked everything that I had just painstaking jammed into the trunk.

"O.K., now let's see you do any better."

The problem is she usually can. She's really good at packing; I'm not. I watched in fascination as she put everything back and to my amazement, it all did fit with just enough space left over for us to squeeze into the front seats.

"All right," she said. "Now let's go."

And off we went on our first camping adventure.

Our idea was to travel across several states, see a little of the country, and camp along the way. If we liked a spot, we'd stay awhile; if not, we'd truck on down the road. The first campground that we pulled into was nothing really special but it was getting late and we needed to stop for the night. For beginning campers such as we were, setting up the heavy army surplus tent became somewhat of an adventure in itself. After a great deal of effort and some salty language on my part, combined with sage and calming advice from my wife, our temporary edifice was finally up and secure.

Then, it started to rain. It came down in torrents. Pools of water collected in pockets at the top of the canvas tent and its roof began to sag inward. I pushed up against one of these pools to clear it and was pleased to find that the water slid right off and down the sides. I was about to tackle the others when I noticed that right where I had pushed against the canvas fabric there was now a steady drip. I decided that the camping store had rented us a leaky tent.

Once again I pushed against another of the pools of water and to my surprise got the same dripping result. Sometimes I'm a slow learner. We now had two leaks inside our previously bone dry structure.

I said to my wife, "Look at this. The crummy camping store rented us a defective tent."

My wife, who had been busy unpacking some of our stuff, turned and saw what I was doing. "No, no, no!" she said. "Don't touch the inside of the canvas!"

"Why not?" I asked.

"Touching the canvas causes leaks," she said in a tone that suggested most intelligent people were aware of this basic camping fact.

I had never heard of this phenomenon before and so, naturally, had to test this new information by pressing against still another spot on the canvas roof. To my amazement she was right, and so now we had a third steady drip in the roof of our tent. Really annoyed now, she explained that with canvas material the surface tension of the water prevents leaks from developing. Touching the material from the inside of the tent breaks the surface tension and causes the leaks. Who knew? I was never a scout. She was.

My punishment for this gap in my camping education was to move my sleeping bag over to the now leaking wet part of the tent while my wife moved into the drier untouched piece of canvas real estate.

The following morning, after a wet and miserable night and a somewhat meager breakfast, we packed up our soggy abode and prepared to hit the trail once again. I decided this putting up and taking down the tent would need some getting used to. Being essentially a non-camper it seemed to me like a lot of wasted effort.

I suggested to my wife, "Why don't we just find a spot on the planet that we like, put up the tent and leave it up until it's time to go home."

"Don't be so lazy. You can't see much of the country stuck in one place. Just drive," she said.

And so down the road we went once again.

The next campground that we pulled into was located in a deep wooded area. The place seemed a little spooky, possibly because we were the only campers there. The tent went up a little faster this time now that we had at least some idea of how to do it.

I took pride in building a small campfire over which my wife prepared a simple but surprisingly good dinner. I began to think that maybe this camping stuff was not going to be so bad after all. After dinner I tucked myself into my comfortable sleeping bag while my wife decided to read a little before going to sleep. I was almost in dreamland when my wife shook me.

"What is it?" I asked, annoyed. "I'm trying to sleep."

Her eyes wide, mouth open, wordlessly she pointed to the wall of the tent. Silhouetted on the outside of the canvas was the biggest bug that I had ever seen. Honestly, it had to be over a foot long. Its antennae waved rhythmically back and forth as it clung to the outside of the tent. Each of its jointed legs was at least as thick as my finger.

"Go outside and kill it," she begged.

My immediate manly response was, "Are you crazy? Look at the size of that thing. It looks prehistoric. Heck, it might even be prehistoric."

I knew a little bit about nature mostly from reading and watching T.V. Not only had I never seen an insect that big but I had never even heard of any creepy crawly growing to such an enormous size. If anyone could ever catch a bug like that they could probably get rich selling it to a museum.

"Please go out and kill it," my bride piteously implored once again.

Bravely holding my ground against a terrified woman I declared, "Not me!"

Seeing that my fright was as least as great as hers, she finally gave up.

"Then what are we going to do?"

At a loss for an answer it was at that moment that I made a major marriage saving discovery and announced, "You can stop worrying about it. It's not a problem."

"Not a problem?" she hissed. Pointing at the enormous bug which was now starting to creep along the canvas she said, "It's moving. What in the world are we going to do if it gets in here?"

Deciding, at the risk of life and limb, that I'd better not keep my discovery from her any longer, I merely pointed at the propane lantern that was hanging from the top of the tent pole.

"What?" was all she asked.

"Don't you see it?" I said.

"See what?" she angrily demanded again.

Then she saw what I had just discovered. There, on the glass of the propane lantern was a tiny little gnat. The light from the lantern projected a perfect foot long shadow of the critter on the wall of the tent as if by a slide projector. Every detail of the diminutive bug was magnified against the impromptu movie screen of the canvas tent. We had been terrified by the projected shadow of an insect so small we could barely see it with the naked eye. Vastly relieved, we began to laugh at the situation and ourselves.

## *Beetle Mania*

Our laughter was interrupted by an inch long black beetle with three red spots on its back crawling across the floor of the tent.

As usual, my wife reflexively demanded, "Kill it."

A bug this small I could handle. "No need for violence," I told her, as I deposited the little critter gently outside of the tent.

"I don't know if I can sleep here if we have beetles," she declared.

"It's just a little insect. We're in the woods. You're the one that wanted to go camping, remember?" I reminded her. "Go to sleep. There's been too much talk about bugs anyway. Now, good night!"

"All right," she said and settled down in her sleeping bag. I was just about to turn off the propane lantern when, crawling across the floor came a second identical black beetle with three red spots on its back.

"That's it," announced my bride as I released it outside. "The tent is infested with beetles. I can't sleep here tonight."

When she gets like this there is only one thing for a loving husband to do: LIE.

I informed her, "Listen, Honey, I know all about this kind of beetle. They travel in mated pairs. Since I just got rid of the mate of the first one you can go to sleep without worrying."

"I know you. You're lying to me", she whined. "You made that up about the pairs."

"No, really," I insisted. "I saw a program about bugs on T.V. and they showed this exact same beetle. They said that most bugs don't mate for life but this kind does."

Not really convinced but willing to be placated, she checked the tent one more time and then reluctantly agreed to turn off the lantern. And then, as luck would have it, she spied a third spotted beetle crossing the floor.

"You see," she exclaimed, "this tent is overrun with them!" As I tossed it outside to join its friends she turned to me and demanded, "Now where is its mate?"

"There is no mate," I admitted. "I just made that up to calm you down."

"Now I know you're lying," she insisted. "There is so a mate and I want you to find it if you have to stay up all night."

I kicked myself for not having the foresight to hold back a spotted beetle in reserve for just such an eventuality. As we searched the tent in earnest I did my best to convince her that I had no more entomological information than she had. Eventually I succeeded and we finally got to sleep. The next day down came the infested tent and we were off to new adventures.

We drove across several states with occasional stops at motels which we knew would provide soft beds and blessedly hot showers. Continuing on we eventually arrived at a remote campsite located in a national park.

## *Big Moe and the Bear*

The campsite was beautiful but really primitive. The only bathroom facilities provided were His and Her adjoining outhouses with no water or electricity. We set up camp, had something to eat and then took a romantic walk together up to the outhouses. As I stepped into the men's side I examined my surroundings. The structure was made of wood and was a one holer. The space was cramped with a very low ceiling. I was about to use the facility when, there in the corner, I spotted a really large bright yellow spider with black markings sitting in the center of a beautiful symmetrical web. The black pattern on its body looked kind of like tiger stripes. It actually was beautiful in a terrifying sort of way.

This critter was not nearly as big as Godzilla had been but it was still big enough to worry about. In fact, it was large enough so that I gave it a name. I called him Big Moe. Later I thought that it probably was a female because in the spider world the females are usually larger. But since that was the first name that popped into my head, Big Moe was it.

Unlike Godzilla, this one was a web spider. I knew that web spiders generally stay at home. Because they live in their web and eat there they don't usually have a reason to go anywhere else. Since I had no choice but to use the facility while we were at the campsite, I decided to make an uneasy truce with Big Moe. If he didn't bother me I certainly did not plan to bother him.

Once back at the tent I told my wife about who I had discovered inhabiting the men's side of the facility. She said it was lucky for Big Moe that he was not on the women's side because she would have insisted that I either immediately kill him or we would have to leave the campground in search of a spider free ladies room. She carefully examined the women's side to assure herself that none of Big Moe's friends or relatives was lurking there.

That night, after dinner, a park ranger came to our camp site and told us that a large bear had been seen in the camping area just days before. He warned us to lock all of our food in the trunk of our car so as not to attract Old Smokey. We did as instructed and prepared to turn in for the night.

By now it was dark and we decided to go up to the facility together one final time before bed. Since the outhouses had no electricity my wife insisted that I first use our only flash light to verify that no spiders had entered the women's side since her last visit. She was not about to occupy a pitch black outhouse without first making absolutely certain that she was in there by herself. Eventually satisfied, my bride graciously allowed me to keep the flashlight so that I could check on Big Moe.

I opened the door to the Men's side and stepped into the dark interior. I shined the light in the corner to make sure that Big Moe was right where he was supposed to be. The symmetrical web was still there but nobody was home. Big Moe had gone.

But where? There was no way that I was going to take another step until I was sure where that very big spider with the tiger stripes had disappeared to. I began to search by shining the light at the web and working my way out slowly and systematically from that point. I played the light carefully over each nook and cranny so as to be sure not to overlook him. I had almost finished my search with no success when I suddenly had a terrifying premonition. All at once I knew exactly where Big Moe was.

It wasn't because I had seen him. I can't explain how I knew. I just knew. The ceiling of the outhouse was very low. As I shined the light directly over my head there was Big Moe, clinging to the ceiling, six inches over my nose. We were suddenly face to face. We made eye contact for a moment; my two and his eight. He was so close that I could have kissed him on the cheek, that is if a spider had a cheek. I have to say that what happened next was not one of my finer or prouder moments. I couldn't help it. I let out an ear piercing screech and sprinted out the door.

Meanwhile my wife, who was comfortably seated next door, knew nothing of all this. All she heard was her husband shout and the sound of footsteps hurriedly retreating in the distance. I didn't think to inform her that it was a spider that had prompted me to yell. I figured that I could explain my Arachnid Adventure when she was finished at the Lady's side and returned to our campsite. There was a full moon so the path back to camp was well lit.

But my wife, hearing me cry out, was sure that the bear that the Ranger had warned us about had returned. She also was convinced that I had abandoned her and left her to fend for herself against the vicious beast. Afraid to open the door and allow the bear to come inside she sat there in the dark for another half hour. In hopes that I would come back to rescue her, every few minutes she quietly called my name. Finally, unable to stay in the Ladies' side any longer and thinking that the bear must have gone, she decided to take a risk and return to camp.

In the meantime I knew nothing about the bear fantasies that she was having and I had just about decided to find out what was taking her so long when she entered the tent.

To say that she was enraged at me would be the grossest of understatements.

"How could you have left me to that bear!" she demanded.

"Bear, what bear?" I asked puzzled.

"I heard you screech and then you ran away. If it wasn't a bear then what was it?" she demanded again.

"It was Big Moe. I looked up and he was right over my face. I got scared and yelled," I informed her.

Incredulous, she responded, "You left me sitting up there for a half hour in a jet black outhouse with no flashlight thinking that a bear was about to break down the door any minute because of a little spider?"

Putting up the best defense I could at the moment I weakly answered, "Big Moe isn't so little."

The chilly air outside was balmy compared to the frost that I endured inside our tent all through that long night. There was no denying the fact that I, like Little Miss Muffet, had been frightened away by a mere spider. Still, despite my somewhat less than heroic behavior, I somehow managed to convince my new bride that a loving husband, such as myself, would cheerfully have done hand to paw combat in her defense with a marauding bruin should the need have arisen. She, on the other hand, drove home the point that clear communication in all future such circumstances was essential for continued marital bliss. Fortunately, as they say, time heals and now we laugh at Big Moe and the Bear.

As to our outdoor adventures, I'm happy to report that there were no more encounters with eight legged marauders. It turned out that camping wasn't so bad after all. We even took many camping vacations for years afterward. When our children were old enough they really loved those trips and, I must say, I got to enjoy them as well.

When we decided to purchase our own camping equipment my wife also acquired a new category of shopping that she liked to do. Each year she added to our collection until we had accumulated so much camping stuff that in an emergency we probably could have outfitted an army platoon. These days however, we don't do much camping anymore. Our kids grew older and developed other interests: the girl in boys and the boy in girls. We got older too. The lure of sleeping on the hard ground and picking bugs out of our morning scrambled eggs had less appeal with the passing years. But it sure was fun while it lasted.

# Zeesa

When my wife and I were first married we lived in an apartment on the sixth floor of a Brooklyn building. Before our children arrived and occupied most of our free time and attention we would occasionally rescue stray dogs that came our way. We really didn't go looking for them; they just seemed to happen by. Once we came home after work to find a large mixed breed dog lying across our welcome mat. This pooch had been wandering up and down between the floors of our building for two days until it ended up at our door. None of our neighbors had seen fit to call anyone or help the poor thing. So it was left to us to do for him what we had previously done for several others.

We took him to the vet for the required exam and shots. He got a bath and we took care of him until we could arrange to find him a good home. We placed an ad in the newspaper and in a relatively short time we received several calls from people interested in adopting him. It seems that most people will readily accept a dog from another person but are reluctant to take the steps that we so willingly took in those days.

This particular mutt was the least grateful of all the dogs that we had previously helped. I took him out for a walk one afternoon when I met one of my neighbors and stopped to talk for a moment. As I was standing there engrossed in the conversation, all of a sudden I felt that my leg was wet. I looked down and was shocked to see that this mongrel was showing his appreciation for being rescued by using my leg for a fire hydrant. When we delivered him to his new owner I must confess that I failed to mention this slight flaw in his personality.

Although what we had been doing for these dogs was personally satisfying, it was very time consuming and all the trips to the vet were getting expensive. So my wife and I agreed to close down our rescue mission for a while.

A while turned out to be just one short week later. My best friend owned a picture frame store and I would often visit him. On this particular day we were standing in front of his shop when a movement at the end of the block caught my attention. A medium sized stray dog was plodding down the sidewalk as if it were walking the last mile. In the direction it was going it would have to cross a very busy wide street and the likelihood of it being hit by one of the speeding cars was great.

The dog was very dirty and looked like it had been homeless for a long time. It seemed exhausted as it dragged itself painfully down the sidewalk. As it got close I commented to my friend, "That's the saddest looking dog I've ever seen. I can't let it cross that busy avenue."

My friend, a really good but tough guy said, "It got this far. Let it go."

"I can't do that; it could get run over."

There was a small grocery store on the corner. I raced inside and got the store keeper to quickly cut a large chunk of baloney for me. I rushed outside again just as the dog was almost to the busy avenue. I walked around in front of the dog and blocked its way. It stopped and seemed barely able to raise its head to see what I was up to. I knelt down and offered it the large chunk of baloney. The stray wolfed the meat down in two quick bites. It obviously had not eaten in a very long time.

Now was the hard part. I intended to take the pooch home with me. But the big question was how to get this stray over to my car. The dog didn't know me. It had no collar and I had no leash or rope. There was a real danger that I could be bitten. I gingerly petted the dog a couple of times. Exhausted, it did not respond either aggressively or with appreciation. I decided to take a chance. I guessed its weight at about thirty pounds as I put both my arms underneath its chest and belly and carefully lifted. The dog made no move to resist, either out of trust or exhaustion; I couldn't tell. I carried it back to my car and gently placed it on the back seat. All the while my friend continued to tell me to let the dog go on its way.

I needed to inform my wife that we were back in the rescue business so I went inside my friend's store to call her. I didn't get quite the response that I expected. It seemed that she was enjoying her new found freedom from our canine rescue squad and was reluctant to give up her free time.

"Don't you dare bring another stray home with you!"

"Too late," I told her, "I can't leave it. It's the saddest pooch you ever saw and it's already in the car."

"I'm warning you; you'd better not," she threatened.

"Listen, Honey. We'll do for this one what we did with the others and quickly find a home for it."

The loud click on the other end of the line told me that my bride was neither convinced nor particularly happy with me.

Being an experienced married man, I remained at my friend's shop for another half hour until I figured that my wife had enough time to cool off. When I got back to my car I saw that the dog was exactly in the same position that I had left it thirty minutes earlier. It had not moved a single muscle in all of that time. The poor thing was totally spent. I felt that I was on a mission of mercy and the wrath I would be facing at home was a small price to pay to save a life.

As I pulled away from my friend's store he called after me, "I'm telling you, you're making a mistake taking that mutt home!"

Once my wife actually saw the stray dog she relented somewhat. When you looked past the dirt, she (it was a female) was really cute. She had floppy ears and was mostly brown with a white muzzle dotted with small brown spots that looked like freckles. Although the dog had obviously been traumatized she appeared to have a mellow disposition. I told my wife that once we cleaned up the dog we should have no trouble finding her a good home.

The thing that we couldn't figure out was how come this dog's ribs were sticking out but she still had a big belly. We decided that the dog must have worms and the vet could easily take care of that.

"This pooch is pregnant," announced our vet as we both stood stunned in his examining room. "I'd say she's due to give birth in about three weeks."

"Pregnant! How can she be pregnant?" my wife and I exclaimed in unison.

"Oh, in the usual way," answered our vet with only the hint of a smile.

"Great. That's just great. It's tough enough to find homes for these strays as it is, but I doubt that we're going to have a lot of luck convincing anyone to take in one that's about to have puppies!"

The vet said the dog was in surprisingly good health considering it had been on the street for some time. She showed no aggression at all during the exam and, aside from the coming blessed event, our veterinarian felt that she'd make someone a very good pet.

We left the dog to be professionally bathed while we went home to discuss our options.

"Listen." I said to an overwrought wife as I attempted to minimize things. "We'll keep the dog for three weeks. Then it'll be just six more weeks until the puppies are weaned and can be given away. It won't be so bad."

She responded with the negative spin she usually reserves to negate my positive one. "Not so bad, huh? You do realize that nine weeks is over two months that we'll have this responsibility?"

"O.K., O.K. So it's over two months but that's not the end of the world. We can survive two months can't we?"

"Sure we can survive, but we wouldn't have to just survive if you hadn't brought home a pregnant stray after we agreed no more rescues for a while!"

The atmosphere between us was just a tad strained as we returned to the vet to pick up our latest house guest. When they brought her out to us we couldn't believe it was the same dog. Her fur was all fluffed up and shiny. She even carried herself differently. She was now wagging her formerly droopy tail like a happy flag. After her bath she was absolutely beautiful. My wife thawed out somewhat at this magical canine makeover.

As the dog licked her hand my wife turned to me and said, "She's really sweet. Maybe it won't be so bad after all."

Once we were back at our apartment we naturally began to show the dog a lot of attention and fatten her up. After all, she was eating for two or three or, well, the vet couldn't exactly tell how many pups were soon to arrive. It had been my experience that most rescued strays are grateful and this one responded to each kind gesture with unbounded love and affection. Although our intention was to find her a new home we had to call her something while she was staying with us.

Zeesa is a Yiddish word that I'd often used and loosely translates to mean, "Sweetheart." So I just fell into the habit of calling her that because it seemed to fit her perfectly. So Zeesa it was. We soon learned that besides being cute and affectionate she was really smart. She learned her new name almost instantly and soon comfortably settled in to our family's routine.

As Zeesa's due date got closer the problem of where this upcoming birth should take place needed to be decided. As I left the apartment building one afternoon I came upon a large refrigerator packing carton that had just been set out for the trash. As if on cue one of our neighbors had thoughtfully purchased a new refrigerator and in so doing provided us with the perfect makeshift puppy nursery.

I wasted no time in wrestling the huge cardboard box into the elevator and dragged it into our apartment. After a little surgery on the carton with a razor knife we had the perfect puppy birthing center. We shifted some furniture around and installed the carton along one wall of our bedroom. After lining the box with old blankets we were ready for the blessed event.

My best friend called to see how we were making out with the dog that he had so strongly advised me to leave on the street. When I informed him about the soon to be arriving puppies he gave me the, "I told you so treatment." He felt that I had taken on an unnecessary burden.

I, on the other hand, was really glad that I had made the decision that I did. I shuddered to think of Zeesa wandering around the city in her condition. I was sure that even if she had survived crossing that busy avenue where I found her, giving birth on the street would have doomed Zeesa and her puppies as well.

My friend's wife, however, saw our upcoming blessed event as an ideal opportunity to teach her six-year-old daughter about the birds and the bees first hand. She asked us to call her when the dog was about to deliver. All that remained now was for Zeesa to do her thing. And two and a half weeks later, exactly on schedule, she did. Six beautiful puppies were born in our bedroom delivery room with no problems and my friend's daughter got the lesson on babies that her mother wanted.

Four of the pups had Zeesa's brown and white markings, one was white with all black accents, and one was pure snowball white. Zeesa was a very mixed breed and her puppies, in all their variety, were just gorgeous.

Nature is wonderful. She knew just how to take care of them and they knew exactly where to get breakfast, lunch and dinner. In the beginning, like all babies, they slept most of the time. After their eyes opened they tended to whine whenever their mother left the nursery carton. After a few weeks, when they got their puppy teeth, they began to clamor for their mothers' attention whenever she was away. Those teeth were sharp and Zeesa naturally became less and less enthusiastic about nursing them. It was time to begin feeding our charges puppy food. To keep the carton clean we fed them outside of the nursery box.

They attacked the food dish like six greedy little hogs. The black and white puppy was the clumsy one of the group. Once when his five brothers and sisters had crowded around the breakfast bowl and there was no room for him, he took a running start, crashed into the puppy pack, flew into the air, and landed upside down in the food dish with a surprised look on his face. His breakfast had to be postponed for a much needed bath.

Whenever they were liberated from the carton the puppies all behaved like escaped convicts. They ran all over our bedroom, attacked our slippers, had mock puppy fights and in general had a great time of it. We were really enjoying them as well. Nothing can put a smile on a person's face faster than a pack of carousing puppies.

That is as long as the supply of paper towels held out. Naturally these babies were too young to be housebroken so, once liberated from the nursery, there seemed to be puppy puddles everywhere. We decided that the almost continuous cleanup we needed to do was a small price to pay for all the fun we were having.

But the puppies were growing fast and the day finally came when they were big enough to escape the nursery carton on their own and fled to all parts of the apartment. Now they were teething in earnest and there were all kinds of things for them to chew on that we didn't especially want chewed. As much as we loved them, since they were fully weaned, it was time to find new homes for the pups.

My wife and I decided that our puppies needed to grow up in a better neighborhood than we lived in. No apartment dwelling for our pampered pups. These guys each deserved a suburban home with a yard. Lucky for them and for us, it was a week before Christmas. What better present could there be for a kid than a new puppy. So we loaded Zeesa and her babies into our car and headed out for the fanciest mall in the most affluent part of New Jersey that we could find.

Once we arrived at our destination we wasted no time in setting up our canine adoption center on the sidewalk outside of the mall. I had made a sign that read, 'Puppies For Free to Loving Home'. We sat down on the beach chairs that we had brought and waited with anticipation. In a surprisingly short time we began to draw a large crowd interested in the pups. We had just about placed the first of the puppies when a security guard showed up and asked us to move.

He said that we had unknowingly set up too close to where a Pet Shop was located inside the Mall. The shop owner was naturally upset that we were giving away outside his store exactly what he was selling inside. The guard was nice about it as he explained that we didn't have to leave the grounds of the mall. We just had to move away from the Pet Shop. So we packed up the puppies and did as instructed. I don't know what the Pet Shop owner thought as the large crowd of potential customers followed us to our new location further down the sidewalk as if we were the Pied Piper.

It seemed everyone wanted a free puppy. But we weren't here just to give them away. Each prospective puppy recipient was strictly interviewed by my wife and me before we deemed them suitable to receive one of our treasured pups.

The clumsy white and black puppy went to a working man with two young children at home. He had come to the mall for Christmas presents for his kids and was lucky enough to come upon us before beginning his shopping. I told him that this cute puppy would rapidly grow into a dog, and asked him if he was sure that his wife wouldn't throw a fit as he walked in the door with a canine surprise. He assured me that he was the master of his household and all would be well at home. We had to trust that he was at least half right.

The next lady wasn't so fortunate. She inquired about the puppy she was interested in, "Does the puppy have to come indoors at all or could it live outside in a doghouse over the winter?"

After several more disturbing questions like that my wife said to her, "I'm sorry, all of the puppies are spoken for."

As the woman was walking away I turned to my wife and asked, "Why did you tell her that? You know that the puppies aren't spoken for."

"There is no way that woman is going to get one of Zeesa's babies. Besides all of the upsetting questions she asked, did you notice she never once even picked up a single one of the puppies? Anyone who can resist petting a puppy is not going to get one from me." I was impressed with my wife's perception. The fact that the woman had not so much as touched any of the pups had totally escaped me.

Our next potential customer was a white-haired grandmother accompanied by an adorable granddaughter of about seven. The child picked up the all white pup we had nicknamed Snowball and it was instant love at first sight. The grandmother watched her grandchild interact with Snowball for a minute but had difficulty making up her mind.

"Are you going to be here every day?" she inquired.

"Well, I certainly hope not."

And then she asked me a question that to this day makes me wonder what goes on in the minds of some people. "Is this your business?"

I was standing next to my large homemade sign as I answered. "Lady, let's read the sign together: Puppies for Free to Loving Home." I couldn't resist adding, "Just how much profit do you think there is in giving away free puppies?"

She thought about this for a moment and said, "All right, we'll take it." I watched the little girl kissing and hugging Snowball as she walked away and it was clear that he was destined for a happy and pampered life.

In just over an hour all the other puppies were adopted and we were content that we had done the best we could for each of them. When we returned home the apartment seemed strangely quiet without the puppy chorus that we had gotten so used to. As to Zeesa, it was now time to find a home for her as well. We really did not want the responsibility of a permanent pooch, but Zeesa truly was a sweetheart. With each passing day we had gotten more and more attached to her. Although we had resolved to find her a good loving home once her puppies had been placed, in the end the most loving home we could think of for this wonderful dog was our own.

The Vet had estimated her age to be two or three and Zeesa lived with us for another twelve years. She loved everyone and everyone loved her with one notable exception. When my best friend came to our house Zeesa would furiously bark and growl at him.

"That dog really hates me," my friend would say during those visits.

I used to tease him by observing that a dog is really a good judge of character and maybe she knew something about him that we didn't. We couldn't understand what was going on to set her off like that. My friend was a biker and always wore heavy motorcycle boots. My wife thought that his noisy stomping around the house may have frightened Zeesa and prompted her aggression toward him.

I had a different idea. Zeesa was one very smart dog. I believe it wasn't the sound of my buddy's heavy boots that upset her. I'm convinced she remembered he was the one who told me not to take her in. I had no other satisfactory explanation as to why Zeesa, who loved everybody, hated my best friend until the day she went to doggie heaven. Those two might not have gotten along but as for me, Zeesa was the best dog I ever had!

# The Grass Is Always Greener

Many years ago we purchased a house on Long Island. It was located in a charming neighborhood lined with mature trees and beautifully manicured lawns. The buzzing of gardeners could be heard like so many giant bees, tending to what appeared to be a host of personal putting greens. The suburban homeowners all seemed to be competing in their number one sport: the pursuit of perfect grass.

Our home, while modest, was bought with what I'm sure at that time must have been our last penny. "I can't afford a gardener," I thought, "so I'll just have to deal with the lawn myself." Having grown up in an apartment in Brooklyn, I figured, "How hard can it be to grow grass anyway?"

Since we had moved in the late fall I couldn't wait for warm weather to get started. The winter seemed to drag on and on but when spring finally did arrive I was excited to see my grass come up thick and beautiful. I rushed out and bought a lawn mower and proudly joined the ranks of my fellow suburbanites. What a joy it was to cut my grass for the first time. I carefully crisscrossed the yard until I had achieved a perfect billiard table look.

As I stood admiring my handiwork an elderly neighbor ambled over and introduced himself. He looked at my expanse of green carpet-like grass with approval.

"Your lawn looks great," he said and ambled away. Wow, I had just received the official suburban seal of approval.

The next day, as I was leaving for work, I noticed near the walkway a small brown spot on the lawn. Not thinking much of it I went off to work only mildly concerned. You have to expect a slight flaw here and there in anything. After all, nothing is perfect. When I returned home from work I knelt down on the lawn to inspect the brown spot more closely. Was it my imagination or had it grown larger in my absence? I went into the house, got involved with family stuff, and promptly forgot about the lawn.

The following morning I was alarmed to see that a second spot had joined the first. I resolved that I would go to the garden center that weekend and find out about these mysterious invaders. By Saturday the lawn had acquired two more. Four brown spots on my perfect grass I decided was four too many. Now truly alarmed, I hurried to the garden center for a quick solution to my lawn problem.

The man at the garden store listened to my description and announced soberly, "You have Brown Spot."

"I know. I just told you that. But what is it?"

He patiently explained, "Brown Spot is the name of a fungus disease that attacks some lawns when they get too much moisture and this has been an unusually wet spring."

"A fungus! Yuck," I exclaimed. "I can get rid of it can't I?"

"Well, Brown Spot is very difficult to deal with. Go down to aisle seven and get the fungus treatment in the small green bottle. That works fairly well but there are no guarantees."

A trip down aisle seven was an education into all the things that could go wrong with grass. I had no idea that lawns were so vulnerable to such a variety of ailments. The thought occurred to me that grass grows naturally on The Great Plains for mile after mile. Nobody mows it. Nobody tends it. It just grows with no problems at all. It was just my luck to get a fungus on my tiny plot of suburbia. I continued down aisle seven feeling really sorry for myself until I spotted the fungus treatment on the top shelf. It was a surprisingly small bottle. I usually don't read labels but being in unfamiliar territory this time I did. The print was hard to read but I managed to decipher the fact that contained within the tiny bottle was concentrate strong enough to make several gallons of fungus treatment. The cost for this lawn salvation was twenty-five dollars. I decided that no price was too high to save my perfect grass. I was moving toward the checkout counter when the word "Caution," printed on the label in red, caught my eye. "Wear eye protection when spraying," it said. "May cause irreversible blindness." Blindness!

I desperately wanted a nice lawn but I had no intention of risking my vision to have one. I carefully put the lethal green bottle back on the shelf before I dropped it, potentially blinding everyone in the store. I approached the clerk once again.

"That fungus remedy you recommended is too scary for me."

"I know, the blindness warning puts some people off."

"Do you have any other suggestions?"

"Well, the only other thing that you can do is rake up the dead grass as the fungus kills it off and plant new grass seed."

So, all through the rest of the spring and into the summer I did battle with the fungus. I diligently raked up every bit of dead grass and reseeded as instructed. I covered the seed with topsoil which I bought from the garden center. I endured ridicule from my mother-in-law, who lived in Maryland farm country. She was sure that I had lost my mind when she found out that her son-in- law was now out buying dirt. She told me that if I drove the six hours to her house she'd give me all the dirt I wanted for nothing. Slings and arrows aside, undeterred I pressed on, but to no avail.

The brown spots grew larger and multiplied like, well, fungus. The blight killed the grass faster than I could rake it up. No amount of new seed, water or fertilizer could keep pace with the devastation.

My wife, at some point, gently suggested that we hire a professional gardener. I employed the "it's too expensive" gambit. She countered with the fact that all the money that I had already spent on a mower, rakes, seed, fertilizers and, last but not least, dirt would have more than paid for the most expensive professional gardener in the neighborhood. I always hate it when she's right but I was committed, and so pressed valiantly on with my battle against the dreaded fungi.

By the end of the summer, my previously beautiful green lawn resembled a large slice of moldy bread. The fall was no better. My anguish dissipated somewhat as we moved into winter when the occasional blanket of snow covered my failed attempts at lawn care.

When spring arrived, refreshed and determined, I dutifully began again. I raked the ground until all signs of dead grass were gone and only the virgin earth remained. I blanketed the soil with a dense layer of the most expensive grass seed I could find and lovingly covered each and every grain with a thin topping of rich top soil. I dutifully watered, said a little prayer and low and behold, awoke one morning to a yard full of baby grass. The immature blades looked like green fuzz but they all seemed healthy and full of promise. I tended my crop faithfully and by mid spring my beautiful lawn was back. I was elated. I could once again hold my head up in the ranks of the other suburban homeowners. The grass really was looking lush, maybe even better than before. I went to bed each night a truly happy man.

One morning as I stood admiring the fruits of my labors, the same elderly neighbor from the year before walked over and observed once again, "Your lawn looks great." And he ambled away.

The following day, on the way to the car, I couldn't restrain a feeling of pride as I stopped to gaze at my perfect grass. It hadn't been easy but I had done a really fine job. Wait! What was this? Were my eyes playing tricks or did I detect a tiny brown spot right in the middle of my yard. I nervously walked over for a closer look. I knelt down and examined it carefully. No amount of wishful thinking could change the fact. The little brown spot was identical to the one that began all the trouble the previous spring. The fungus was back. I was devastated.

Why had this plague arrived only on my property when all around me were perfect lawns? A fleeting thought occurred to me. Maybe it was my elderly neighbor's fault. Maybe he had put a hex on my lawn. Maybe the old guy was jealous because his grass was not as perfect as mine. Had he given my property the evil eye or something? He did not appear to have that kind of power, but the timing was very suspicious. For two consecutive seasons the brown spots appeared just one day after he had admired my lawn. I knew that the idea of a hex was far-fetched but I had to consider all the possibilities.

Once again I rushed to the garden center. Behind the counter was a different clerk than I had spoken to the previous year.

"I did everything the other guy said but the fungus is back!"

The clerk told me that once fungus attacks a lawn it's very difficult to get rid of without serious chemical treatment.

"You mean the stuff that causes blindness?"

The clerk gave me a puzzled look. Obviously he hadn't read the label.

"Is the fungus treatment in the little green bottle the only thing that works?"

"Usually, but there are no guarantees."

I left the store in a state of agitation as I pondered this bit of gardening philosophy. Lawns, like life it seems, do not come with guarantees.

Back at home I was agonizing over the slow death of my grass, which I knew from bitter past experience I was incapable of preventing. While reading the local paper I spotted a classified ad that offered some hope. The small headline proclaimed, "Expert Lawn Care."

Not thrilled about the potential expense, but also not wanting to be ostracized by the neighborhood's perfect lawn people, I gave in to my wife's suggestion and reluctantly reached for the telephone.

To my surprise the owner of the gardening company answered the phone personally. He sounded very knowledgeable and told me that he could come over in a few days to assess the extent of the problem.

"Can't you get here any sooner? After all, fungus like rust never sleeps. I don't want this blight to get out of hand again before you get here."

In a calm voice the gardener told me that he had other clients that he had to accommodate and assured me that a few extra days would not make any difference.

True to his word the potential savior of my lawn pulled up in front of the house as promised in an SUV towing a small trailer. He was a young man and very well spoken. During our conversation he explained that he didn't have a crew and that he was the entire company. When I expressed some concern over this lack of manpower he responded that it was hard to get good reliable help and it was better for his customers anyway. He claimed that as an expert he could give each of his clients the personal attention they deserved.

"You don't seem like the typical gardener. You sound more like a college professor."

"Well, I used to be one but I didn't like it much. I prefer being outdoors and I enjoy working with my hands." I found it strange that he had given up an academic career but kept this thought to myself. Professor Green, as I'll call him, then took a clipboard from his car and said, "Let's see what we're dealing with here."

I generally have an aversion to trades people who show up with clipboards. It's been my experience that they charge more than those who don't. Professor Green, as it turned out, was no exception. He surveyed my yard and the offending spots. He made copious notes. Finally he was done and turned to me.

"It's Brown Spot all right. Fungus hates bright sun and you have a lot of shade trees covering a good part of the lawn. They help to keep the yard wet. You also are probably over watering the grass as well. Most people who develop brown spot are guilty of overwatering."

"You can get rid of the fungus can't you?"

In response, Professor Green returned to his car and took out several pamphlets on lawn care. The first one he handed me was entitled, "Brown Spot and Other Fungus Lawn Diseases."

"There are others?" I gasped.

"Oh, many different ones. Brown Spot is just one of the more common varieties," he explained. "Read this. It will detail what we're up against."

"I can't believe that simple grass can have this many problems," I observed.

"Have you ever heard of the Law of Entropy?" Professor Green asked.

"No, what's that?" I inquired, feeling suddenly like the dumb kid in the Professor's class.

"The Law of Entropy states that everything is either in a constant state of either breaking down or being attacked by something else," he explained. Noticing my blank look he went on in his best Professorial voice to enlighten me. "Prey animals have their predators. Iron has rust. Wood has rot and termites. Grass has fungus and many other potential problems. Everything breaks down," he repeated again for emphasis. "Everything, even people."

On this cheerful note, which I still worry about to this day, Professor Green produced a contract with a slight of hand that any magician would have envied. I hurried to sign it before any additional calamities descended on my lawn. The contract outlined a long list of services each with a different price tag. I opted for the basic plan which would not reduce my family to a strict diet of peanut butter. The Professor said that he would begin the following week. As I stood on the sidewalk watching him drive away I glanced at the pamphlets that he had given me. I suddenly realized that in an hour long discussion the Professor had never definitely said that he would fix my lawn. Oh well, Professor Green knew more about grass than anyone I had ever met. I was sure that everything was going to be fine.

The next week the Professor began in earnest. First he mowed and edged the lawn. I lamented having spent the money for my own mower which was now gathering dust in the shed. Then, using a garden spreader, he put some granular stuff on the lawn to treat the fungus. When I asked him about the little green bottle touted by the garden center he seemed unfamiliar with that product. I found it a little strange that he didn't know about it but the Professor said that his own methods were just as effective.

When he was done I asked, "The stuff you just put on will fix the problem? I am going to have grass this year, won't I?"

In response, the Professor went on about the care and feeding of lawns. He retrieved several new pamphlets on the subject from his car and handed them to me. He was a veritable fount of information. As we stood there on the sidewalk the Professor held an impromptu seminar on grass in all its aspects. Swept away by his torrent of words once again it went completely unnoticed by me that the one thing he never did say was, "Yes, you will definitely have grass."

Week after week Professor Green arrived at my house and did his thing. The problem was that his thing didn't seem to be working. As the volumes of pamphlets and literature that Professor Green heaped on me grew, so too did the mold. The fungus continued unchecked as it had the year before.

There were now large patches of unsightly dead grass visible in many areas of the lawn. The Professor's sidewalk seminars grew longer and my patience grew shorter. Never once did he say that he would fix the problem for sure. He talked and talked about things like the P.H. and alkalinity of the soil. The soil was everything he proclaimed.

"Well," I told him, "my soil seems to be ideal for growing a bumper crop of fungus."

By the end of the season the lawn resembled a miniature version of the Oklahoma dust bowl. There was virtually no grass left at all. Each time Professor Green pushed his mower across what he now must have envisioned as an imaginary lawn, a large cloud of dust would trail behind him.

When I pointed out to the good Professor that there did not seem to be anything left for him to mow he handed me a brochure outlining his reseeding program. Looking at his price list I felt that I could get away cheaper by just rolling up dollar bills and sticking them in the ground side by side. The results would probably have ended up a whole lot greener besides.

I opted to reseed the lawn myself. I was now back in familiar territory. Reseeding I could do. The professor told me to use peat moss to cover the seed instead of top soil because he said that the moss would retain moisture better and allow the grass to germinate faster.

Peat moss, as I found out, comes packaged in large bales. Since I had to practically reseed the whole yard I bought the largest one the garden center had. Once at home again I set to work. After several hours of raking and seeding I was ready for the easy part, spreading the peat moss. The stuff was very light and fluffy and easy to spread by hand when you crumpled it. A stiff wind was blowing as I covered the grass seed. Thinking nothing of the peat moss particles that had been swirling around me all at once I began to have trouble breathing. Without realizing it I had been inhaling large quantities of the fibrous material.

Abandoning the lawn, I rushed into the house and quickly drank several glasses of water. This didn't help at all and I was now really gasping for air. "Why didn't I wear a dust mask?" I thought. "Why hadn't the professor warned me about this potential problem? And, most importantly, why was I doing this at all anyway? If Professor Green had fixed the lawn in the first place I wouldn't be in this trouble now," I concluded. I vaguely remembered that the lungs often have the capacity to clear themselves. I fervently hoped that this was one of those times.

It took several days but fortunately my breathing eventually returned to normal. I carefully sealed up the unused portion of peat moss and put it out for the trash. I had avoided blindness but almost strangled to death, all for the love of my lawn. Who knew that yard work could be this dangerous?

Once again the grass came up and was promptly consumed in turn by the relentless Brown Spot Fungus. Standing on the sidewalk listening to yet another seminar hosted by Professor Green, I finally had enough. In as gentle terms as I could muster I told him that his services were no longer required. He responded by saying that it sometimes takes several seasons to get a fungus problem under control and that I should hang in there with him. I didn't think that I could bear to be the lone student in Professor Green's grass class for one more minute let alone several more seasons. He just kept talking and talking as if he hadn't heard me fire him.

Finally I did the only thing that I could think of to put an end to the Professor's sidewalk filibuster. I told him that I was out of money and I no longer could afford to pay him for a second season. This lie was uncomfortably close to the truth as I had spent a small fortune on my lawn so far to no avail. When it actually registered on him that I couldn't pay for any future services the good Professor abruptly stopped talking. He packed up his pamphlets and his reference materials and drove off into the sunset leaving me alone to contemplate my fungus patch. Well, at least I still had my health, barely.

What to do now? Maybe I was just not destined to have a lawn. "A rock garden wouldn't look so bad," I thought. "At least you never have to reseed it."

I filed this thought away as a possibility. Then, walking my dog around the neighborhood I began to notice that the houses with the best looking lawns were all tended by the same garden company. Several days later they showed up on my block to service the property of one of my neighbors. His lawn always looked fantastic.

I approached the gardening crew and spoke with a short, middle aged Italian man who, it turned out, was the owner of the company. I introduced myself and told him that I had been admiring his work for some time.

"Would you take me on as a client?"

"Sorry," he replied, with a heavy accent, "I have too many customers already."

"Please, you're on the block once a week anyway. You don't even have to use any extra gas to get to my place," I pointed out.

He thought for a minute and then finally agreed to service my lawn. I felt as if I had just been accepted into a prestigious fraternity.

There was just one thing though. I needed to explain about the fungus problem. If Professor Green with all of his education couldn't handle it, maybe this fellow wouldn't even want to try. He listened patiently as I described the problem. Then I asked him the all important question, "Am I going to have a lawn like my neighbors? Will I actually have grass?"

Without any hesitation he answered with a single word, "Sure!"

And magically, I did. I don't know what he put on the lawn or how he accomplished it. But he and his crew worked a grassy miracle seemingly overnight. No pamphlets, no sidewalk seminars, the man just really knew how to grow grass.

We owned that house for many years. In that time my lawn and I made an uneasy peace with each other. I no longer obsessed over it and the lawn stopped growing fungus with the help of my Italian friend. I came to realize, albeit a little late, that there are more important things in life than perfect grass. Things like eye sight, breathing and time off from yard work to be with the family. Oh yes, it turned out that my elderly neighbor hadn't put a Hex on my yard after all. So each spring, when he made his annual trip across the street to admire my lawn I just thanked him politely and walked away.

# A Day At The Beach

Some years ago my mother-in-law bought a summer home on the eastern shore of Maryland. This was a modest cottage located at the mouth of the Wicomico River on the Chesapeake Bay. The Wicomico is so wide at this point that you can't see across to the other side. Because of its close proximity to the bay, this section of the river even had a high and a low tide. The setting was very beautiful and seemed idyllic.

That is until the sun went down and hordes of the largest salt marsh mosquitoes that I have ever seen rose up to attack every living thing. Undaunted, my mother-in-law loved the place and quickly proceeded to make mosquito netting for each of the beds. When it was time for sleep I felt as if I was starring in a jungle movie. When anyone complained about the squadrons of flying bloodsuckers, she responded that the local people liked the bugs because they helped to keep the developers away. She may have had a point. The mosquitoes were ably assisted in their campaign against the evil developers by legions of both horseflies and green-head flies that made their appearance seasonally. Relief was not always available by taking refuge in the water either, as flotillas of stinging jellyfish also made regular visits at the waterfront.

But numerous and sundry vermin aside, this was blue crab country. My mother-in-law, who had somewhat of a reputation for frugality, lost no time putting out two commercial crab traps which she tied to the end of the dock. These traps worked overtime and provided a seemingly endless supply of crab meat for the table. Crab was to be the staple food of the cottage throughout the summer. This delicacy was prepared in a variety of ways and was served at virtually every meal. Was it because the meat was so tasty or because this bounty from the river cost almost nothing to acquire? Since my mother-in-law had been known to pinch a penny or two, I had my suspicions.

I couldn't resist an uncharitable thought. I wondered, "If she had bought a place next to a dairy farm, would she have set out cow traps to provide us with free unlimited hamburger?" This fleeting reverie I wisely kept to myself.

Also located on the property was a barn-like structure that we called the Boat House because, surprise, surprise, it came with an old boat. Well, sort of a boat. It was an antique aluminum rowboat that was equipped with an ancient three and a half horsepower engine. This venerable craft had three warped wooden seats. Under each was glued a thin piece of Styrofoam which served as make-shift flotation.

I studied the engine carefully. It really was an old timer. A strange looking knob stuck out from the front of the thing. It looked like what you'd see on some washing machines. This, I found out later, was how the engine's carburetor was adjusted. Numbers one to four were printed on it. Each faded digit represented a different speed, four being maximum power. The knob was inventively held in place at number four by a dirty piece of adhesive tape because the original metal spring designed to serve that function had long since rusted away. It was clear why the previous owner had left the rowboat behind.

It probably would have cost more to haul it away than the whole thing was worth.

All of the above considerations aside, the family now had access to waterfront property and a powerboat of sorts. Ah, but I soon learned there was a price to be paid for free vacations. Over the course of time my mother-in-law required visiting members of the family to pitch in and donate whatever skills and expertise they could provide to maintain the aging cottage.

She always had an interesting attitude toward men. It was never voiced but it was clear. She believed that if you were a man, you should and could fix things, all things. It didn't matter to her if you went to school or were trained for that particular skill or not. If you were male that qualified you. Once she asked me if I could fix her television set. When I suggested that a T.V. repairman might be a better candidate for the job, her disappointment in her son-in-law was evident.

A visit to her summer place often meant more work than play. So it should not have come as a surprise when my mother-in-law turned to me one day and casually said, "I need you to build a dock."

"Excuse me!" I gasped. "Did you say a dock?"

"Yes, that's right," she went on, "I need you to replace the one we had that was taken out by the last storm."

"But, but," I protested. "The largest thing that I've ever constructed was a book shelf. I don't know a thing about building a dock."

"Well, then it's about time that you learned," she insisted.

Knowing my mother-in-law as I did, I knew that any further argument was pointless. I was stuck with a job that I had no clue as to how to begin, let alone complete.

So I politely inquired, "Do you have any tools?"

"I have no idea. Look in the boat house."

"How about wood? Do you have any materials to build this… dock?"

"I think that there may be some lying out in the backyard."

With an air of finality, she turned and walked away making it clear that she would have no further involvement in the project until it was completed.

A search of the boat house turned up an ancient hammer with a wobbly head. The few oak boards that I found in the yard had been bleaching in the sun for years and behaved more like iron than wood. They refused to yield even an inch to the dull rusty saw the Boat House also grudgingly provided.

Therefore, I reluctantly went off to the local building supply for tools, nails, wood, pilings and instructions as to how one might satisfy a determined mother-in-law. To my surprise the project turned out to be relatively simple and even fun. The water was shallow and warm. The river bottom was hard sand and sloped gradually. This allowed me to stand in the water and easily place the pilings where I wanted them. My wife and several family members pitched in to help and, after less than a week, there it was. It wasn't pretty. It wasn't exactly straight. But it was undeniably a dock. I was extremely proud of what my crew and I had constructed. Many years later, I still am.

My mother-in-law was also delighted with the results and immediately put the crab traps back to work. She also lost no time in informing me, "I knew that you could do it."

This was not so much a compliment but rather an admonishment not to complain the next time that I was asked to do something.

The dock now completed, I planned a day of complete relaxation. After all, I decided, I had more than earned it. I placed a beach chair at the water's edge and had barely settled in with a cold drink and a warm feeling of accomplishment when my bride approached.

My wife is the type of person who, while not quite a workaholic, is someone who feels that people should be busy and productive most of the time. She has cheerfully said on more than one occasion that there is time enough to rest when you are dead. On the other hand, I am proud to say that I've perfected sloth to the level of an art form. This, as you might imagine, has created somewhat of a compatibility problem in our marriage. She would deny it but, when it comes to me, my wife has what I describe as relaxation radar. All I have to do is put my feet up and she magically appears with some task or other for me to perform. But this time it wasn't just her radar at work. They say the apple does not fall very far from the tree.

Her grandmother, who was also visiting at the cottage, had made a request. She thought that the crabs might be bigger farther out in the river. Grandma wondered if I would take her out in the rowboat to deeper water and the larger crabs.

I loved my wife's grandmother dearly, everyone did. She was the Grand Dame of the family. So I grudgingly got up from the beach chair. Then I glanced at the river. What I saw brought me up short. The river was covered in whitecaps. The flag that we raised each morning was whipping in the wind.

I turned to my wife and said, "Look at the river. Today is not the day to go out in the boat."

"What do you mean not go?" she demanded. "You would deny my grandmother?"

"That's not the point," I protested. "That crummy rowboat shouldn't be motoring around a mill pond let alone a river that big on a day like this."

Then my wife said the only thing that could possibly change the mind of a clear thinking, rational, red blooded man.

"Wimp," she declared, then turned on her heel and marched away.

I slumped back down on the chair and weighed my options. All I had wanted to do was relax a little and now this. I stared at the flag. It was standing straight out from the flagpole. Was it just my imagination or was the wind blowing harder than before? I studied the river more carefully. The white caps definitely seemed larger. I had limited experience with boats. Most of the ones that I had been on were really big and came equipped with captains and knowledgeable crews that knew what they were doing. This was clearly not the case with us. But, "Wimp" was the label that my loving wife had just hung on me and there seemed only one possible way to remove it.

I stomped into the house and faced my bride. "All right, you want to go, let's go," I announced.

Her frosty expression melted into a warm smile. "Thank you. I knew you would see reason."

Unable to resist a final protest, I began, "I still want to go on record as being against this but…"

She silenced me with a kiss and hurried away to get her grandmother.

Off I went to the boathouse. As I stood there contemplating our ancient vessel I spotted an empty coffee can nearby.

"We will definitely need this to bail today," I thought, and tossed it into the bottom of the boat.

The can was soon joined by two gray, weathered oars, just in case our mighty three and a half horse power engine happened to conk out. After hooking up the portable gas tank I decided that we were ready. I couldn't think of anything else to do except haul the thing down to the water's edge. I grabbed the piece of frayed rope that was tied to the bow and, with some difficulty, managed to drag our craft down to the small beach in front of the house.

Wading into the river I launched the boat and climbed in. I was afloat. A quick survey of the bottom revealed no apparent leaks. So far so good. I pulled the cord to start the engine and nothing happened. I pulled harder to no avail. It occurred to me that it might have been years since Old Smoky had last been called to service. Maybe I'd get lucky and the stupid thing was truly dead so we could forget about those mythical Goliath crabs supposedly lurking out in the deeper water. Unfortunately, the engine roared to life on the very next pull of the starter cord. No backing out now.

I guided the rowboat to the end of our brand new dock where my wife and her grandmother were anxiously waiting. We helped Grandma get in and safely seated. Then came the crab nets, the peach basket to hold our catch, and finally my wife.

I noticed, with some concern, that we did not have very much freeboard. For those of you non-nautical types, freeboard is a term used to describe the distance from the water line to the top of the boat. I calculated that, fully loaded as we were, there was probably no more than eight inches separating us from the river.

I was about to share this fact with my wife when my superior officer announced, "All right. Let's go."

With the "Wimp" label still fresh in my mind, I decided to keep mum. I pointed the bow toward the horizon and off we went.

The three and a half horsepower fire breather moved us along at a surprisingly fast pace. As we headed out I glanced back at my passengers. Grandma sat on the middle seat wearing an enormous straw hat for protection from the sun even on this cloudy and overcast day. She held her crab net as if it were a flag. Very relaxed for a non swimmer, she appeared not the least concerned for the weather conditions or the water that occasionally splashed over the bow as we ploughed through some of the larger whitecaps. I realized that Grandma, a lady of impeccable manners, considered herself a guest in our boat and completely trusted in us to provide for her safety. She also didn't seem to notice my wife occasionally bailing some water.

I continued to marvel at how smoothly the ancient engine was functioning. As we traveled further and further from the beach the size and frequency of the whitecaps began to increase. So did the amount of water that continued to slosh over the bow. I anxiously observed that the pace of my wife's bailing efforts was also increasing.

Oh well, she had her job and I had mine. On we naively went. At some point I became aware that the water in the bottom of the boat was getting deeper. I again looked back at my wife. Grim faced, she was frantically trying to keep up with the white caps splashing in but, considering that we were now ankle deep, she seemed to be losing the battle.

As our eyes met she said, "Maybe we should go back?"

This observation may very well rank as one of the understatements of the century.

Barely stifling a shout of joy, I merely replied, without a hint of wimpiness, "All right, if you really want to."

I looked back toward the land and was shocked to see how far we had come. "The Little Engine That Could" had brought us at least a half a mile out from the cottage. With great relief I turned the rowboat around and set our course for the distant shore.

The only problem was that heading out, the pointed bow cut nicely through the approaching waves. As we turned back the waves were now coming at us from behind. This condition is what real sailors refer to as "a following sea". The first big white cap hit the flat back of the rowboat with a loud, "SLAP." Water splashed over the stern and the engine as well. The first casualty was the piece of adhesive tape that had been holding the carburetor adjustment knob in place. I watched in fascination as it floated away. With nothing securing the knob, it began to slip down to the off position. I desperately grabbed for it and frantically twisted it back to number four, full power, right before the engine cut out.

I was now acting in place of that essential piece of tape. The knob was wet and slippery. Even with my limited boating experienced I knew that it was imperative to keep the engine going at all costs. To that end I focused all of my efforts on the task and so it was with great annoyance that I heard my wife calling to me from the bow. Without turning around I waved her off. Once again came her voice calling my name, this time more insistent. Did I detect a note of panic?

I looked at her over my shoulder. "Can't you see I'm busy?" I snapped.

Eyes and mouth wide open she wordlessly pointed to the right corner of the stern. I turned to look and was horrified to see that the corner of the boat was UNDER the river. In the blink of an eye the rowboat completely filled with water and we began to sink. Where were the life jackets? The previous owner of the boat wasn't thoughtful enough to provide them so we hadn't brought any.

People that I've told about this experience have asked if I was terrified. The answer is, for me, there wasn't time. Everything happened so fast and the shock was too great. I don't know about others who might unfortunately find themselves in a similar position, but my first response to our sinking was to deny the fact of it. In a reaction that would have done justice to the old comedy team of Laurel and Hardy, I attempted to maintain my, by now, waist deep position in the water by straightening my legs as the boat sank out from under us. As you might imagine, this approach served me well for all of one second.

Grandma, a non-swimmer at slightly over five feet tall, naturally became terrified and flailed around in a panic still clutching her crab net. My wife put her arm around

Grandma's waist in an attempt to calm her as we continued to sink. And then, suddenly, the boat hit bottom. A half a mile off the beach, I found myself standing in water up to my chin. My wife, who at five ten is almost as tall as I am, could also safely stand. As bad as this was, if the water were only a few inches deeper we would have been in much, much, more serious trouble.

But my wife was not having an easy time keeping her grandmother's head above water as Grandma was still in a panicky state. My wife told her to feel the bottom with the handle of the crab net. Only when Grandma verified that the river in fact had a bottom was she able to relax. Water up to our chins, my wife and I stepped out of the rowboat and assessed our situation. There were no other boats in sight. Out of options, we would simply walk back toward the beach.

To my surprise the rowboat began to slowly rise like some kind of strange sea creature. The few flimsy pieces of Styrofoam that were glued under the seats were not able to keep us afloat but provided just enough buoyancy to get the thing off of the bottom once we stepped out of the boat. I grabbed the bow rope and began to tow our treacherous craft, which now floated a few feet under the surface, back toward the beach. My wife held up her grandmother who was using the crab pole as an improvised walking stick as if to verify that the bottom was still there with every step we took.

Looking back, I've wondered why I just didn't leave our illustrious craft right where it sank. I've since decided that I towed it back to shore because it belonged to my mother-in-law, and therefore I felt responsible for its return. Besides, she probably would have expected me to buy her a new boat had I left it there.

I don't know how long it took to get back but it seemed like forever. Approaching the dock, I saw my mother-in-law anxiously waiting for us. As we made our inglorious landfall she verified that everyone was all right. After she had been properly reassured, I couldn't resist asking, "Didn't you used to be a life saving instructor at summer camps?"

"That's right," she replied.

"So where were you when there was a good chance that we were all going to drown? Why didn't you try and save us?" I demanded.

She quietly responded, "You were too far out for me to swim. I knew that it would be too late by the time that I got to you. I knew that you all had no chance at all if the river was not at LOW TIDE."

Afterward I thought about what I ultimately took away from our sinking the boat. The saying "Sticks and stones may break my bones….." that we've all heard as children came suddenly to mind. Way back then it held no real meaning for me as I recited it in sing-song fashion to ward off any childish insults thrown in my direction. But after our near death experience that childhood ditty suddenly took on deadly serious relevance. So now, whenever I refuse a challenge to do something that I consider inherently dangerous, any label implying cowardice on my part I comfortably wear with pride.

# Hot Fudge

One sunny August afternoon my wife and I decided to take a drive in the country. Accompanying us were my brother, his wife and another couple. It took us some time to escape the city limits and we ultimately found ourselves driving through the rolling hills of Pennsylvania. The countryside was beautiful, but the day turned out to be blisteringly hot. About mid-afternoon we were all hungry and thirsty. So it was with great excitement that we spotted an ice cream parlor at a bend in the road. This did not appear to be just any emporium of ice cream but rather could be described as the quintessential example of its kind.

It stood alone on a large expanse of green lawn surrounded by shade trees and was bordered on all sides by colorful and fragrant flowers. The building looked as if it could have almost been made of gingerbread itself. There were no other cars in the small parking lot as we pulled in. We couldn't wait to exit the car in anticipation of the wonderful treats that we knew awaited us inside.

As we entered the building we inhaled the heady fragrance of vanilla and other tantalizing sweet scents that floated on the air. There was a long cool white marble counter behind which was a completely stocked soda fountain. Refrigerated glass cases displayed an extensive variety of ice cream flavors. Our mouths began to water. In addition to the stools at the counter there were several cabaret style tables at which to sit.

We elected to sit at the counter as the waitress approached. She was a beautiful blonde young woman who appeared to be about college age.

"Welcome to the Sweet Shop," she said, as she handed each of us a menu. "We have a lot of things to choose from so I'll give you a few minutes to decide."

The waitress had vastly understated the scope of the menu. Contained within its pages was just about everything that an ice cream lover could desire. Each of the items had a number listed next to it. We quickly made up our minds and the beautiful waitress carefully wrote down our choices on a little pad. My wife was the last to order.

She said to the waitress, "It's so hard to decide. I like banana splits. I also like hot fudge sundaes. All right, give me a banana split with vanilla ice cream and put some hot fudge on it, please."

The smile abruptly disappeared from the young woman's face to be replaced with an expression of concern. "You…you mean that you want a hot fudge sundae?"

"No," replied my wife, "I'd like a banana split and I want you to put some hot fudge on it."

Her expression now escalated to one bordering on alarm. "I don't know if I can do that. I'll have to go and ask."

The young waitress suddenly turned and left the counter. She pushed open the swinging doors to the kitchen and was gone. All of us sitting at the counter were left wondering, "Where did she go? Who is she asking about the fudge? And why does she need to ask about it anyway?"

All of these questions were soon to be answered as the swinging doors to the kitchen were roughly pushed open. Out of the kitchen came what I can only describe as a troll of a woman. She was short and almost completely round. Her unkempt appearance was heightened by her shapeless wrinkled dress. Greasy grey hair hung down over her scowling face like a wet mop. Behind her followed our previously cheery young waitress. She now had the demeanor of a frightened puppy no doubt anticipating what was to come.

Troll woman approached and demanded in a heavy German accent, "Who Vishes Da Hot Fudge?"

My wife spoke up and the troll woman quickly moved down the counter. She stood in front of my wife and flipped open a menu. She pointed a stubby finger to the hot fudge sundae pictured there which had the number five prominently printed next to it.

"Dis is vat you vish?" she demanded again. Her accent seemed to thicken.

"No," my wife again patiently explained. "As I told the waitress, I would like a banana split with hot fudge on it."

"Impossible!" snapped Troll Woman. "Banana split is number eight. Hot fudge sundae is number five. Vich von do you vant?"

It suddenly dawned on us that to communicate clearly with Troll Woman in her own language you needed to use numbers.

"I would like the number eight and I want hot fudge on it."

Troll Woman reacted as if she had just been assaulted. Her voice rising, she pounded on the beautiful marble counter with a clenched fist.

"No mixing!" she exclaimed. "You vill have number vun or number two or number three…" and she went on to shout out several more numbers on the menu. With each number her German accent seemed to get thicker. Even the blonde waitress, who no doubt had seen this tirade before, shrank back in fear.

All of us at the counter sat dumbfounded not believing what we were witnessing. After all, hadn't we put a man on the moon? What was the big deal with slopping a little fudge on a banana?

Finally, out of breath, Troll Woman was done with her counting fit. Like a crouching tiger she waited for my wife to choose a single number from the menu.

For the sake of peace I interjected, "Listen, I'll tell you what. We'll buy a number eight banana split and we'll also buy a number five hot fudge sundae. You can charge us for both of them. Then just take the fudge from the sundae and put it on the banana split. O.K?"

While this seemed to me to be a reasonable compromise to a ridiculous situation Troll Woman reacted as if she had just heard me declare war on her homeland.

Now shouting in earnest as flecks of saliva flew from her mouth, Troll Woman actually bellowed, "It cannot be done!" This declaration was punctuated by her pounding on the marble counter with such force that I was sure it would shatter at any moment.

Fearing that all of this fudge folly was about to escalate into actual violence at any moment we opted to leave without tasting even a single bite of the Sweet Shop's offerings.

Many years later I saw a much milder version of what we had experienced echoed in the film "Five Easy Pieces". But that was fiction. What we encountered that day in the idyllic looking ice cream parlor unfortunately was all too real.

The hot fudge, as it turned out, was far too hot after all.

# The Funeral

A former head of the A.S.P.C.A. once said that when you acquire a pet you have a tragedy in the making. What he meant was: eventually all the years of companionship that you get from Fluffy or Fido will cause deep sorrow when you finally lose your faithful friend. Most of us feel that the trade-off for all those years of unconditional love is worth it.

I'm a dog person or at least I was until that fateful day when my wife, then my girlfriend, announced to me that when she wasn't around she felt that I needed company.

"I'm getting you a cat," she announced.

"A cat? I don't want a cat. I don't know anything about them. I don't even like cats."

With perfect female logic she retorted, "If you don't know anything about cats then how can you say you don't like them?"

I weakly replied, "I heard they were sneaky and they scratch."

"Nonsense," she responded, and with an air of finality she proclaimed, "I'm getting you a cat."

Needing the final word, I practically shouted, "You'd better not!"

Some days later, I stood on the sidewalk outside of my apartment building when my girlfriend walked up. As we stood talking I noticed a slight movement under her coat. Before I could ask, a smile spread across her face and a tiny kitten's head peaked out at me.

Really annoyed I said, "I told you no cats! You take it right back where you got him."

She sweetly informed me, "she's a her and she came from the pound. Today was her LAST DAY, if you know what I mean. Do you really want me to take her back?"

I looked down at a cute little black and white face. She looked back at me with trusting kitten eyes. Being a person of strong convictions I glared at my girlfriend and said, "All right, give me the damn thing." I picked up the kitten which was only slightly bigger than my hand. She licked my face and I was done.

I named her Serena after my favorite belly dancer. So began a friendship which lasted nineteen years. As she grew, so did the bond between us. I found that Serena wasn't sneaky at all and, like any female, only scratched when upset or provoked. In the years that we spent together I subsequently married my girlfriend and our family increased. We had a daughter and a son and acquired several additional cats. While I try never to play favorites with my children, Serena remained my favorite feline.

In addition to being a loving animal, Serena was the smartest cat we ever had. On one occasion she showed reasoning bordering on brilliance. It happened when I first noticed that Serena had lost interest in the scratching post that we had bought from the pet store. She seemed to have decided that our sofa would make an excellent substitute. No amount of pleading, lecturing or even yelling would dissuade her from applying her razor sharpies to the protesting fabric of our couch. What to do? Upon reflection, I decided that Serena would just have to be barred from the living room.

Off I went to the pet store and returned with what I was sure would be the salvation of our furniture, an accordion style doggie gate. As I set to work Serena sat beside me watching me install the barrier to her chosen scratching post. The job done, with great satisfaction I pulled the gate across the entry to the living room and latched it securely.

I looked down on my feline friend and said, "Sorry old girl but you brought this on yourself."

Serena looked back at me with an expression which can only be described as, "You poor fool." She then stepped through one of the diamond shaped openings of the gate and went right back to work on the sofa. Alas, I had miscalculated on two levels. One, I installed a doggie gate to keep out one very smart cat; and two, I had not considered the size of our living room entryway. By pulling the accordion gate across such a wide span, I had created openings a Panther could have walked through. Somehow I would have to plug those spaces.

Undeterred and on a mission, off I went to the lumber yard. I returned with an armload of furring strips and a box of wood screws. Once again I set to work and once again Serena sat beside me. I painstakingly screwed the wooden strips across each and every opening. I was sure my chubby feline friend would not be able to get through these reduced spaces.

As I worked I noticed that Serena seemed to be studying what I was doing as if she was trying to understand my motivation. I decided that my imagination was playing tricks because cats are not known to have this capacity for reasoning.

Oh, little do we know. After almost an hour I was done. I had created an impenetrable barrier to the living room. However, by screwing the wooden strips across the openings the accordion gate now functioned more like a fixed door. Another miscalculation. Oh well, at least I've saved the sofa I thought.

I stood back and admired my handy work. "Try and get through that," I announced with satisfaction as I latched the gate.

Serena looked up at me as if she understood the challenge. She studied the gate intently.

"Sorry, the living room is now officially off limits."

Ignoring my proclamation, she fixed her attention on the reinforced barrier barring her way. She stared at it as if analyzing the problem. Then Serena did something which to this day I still have trouble believing, and I saw her do it. She stretched out her paw and curled it around one of the strips of wood that I had so carefully screwed to the gate. Out came those razor sharp claws. She looked up at me one more time as if to say, "You can't beat me."

I watched in amazement as she pulled back on the quarter inch thick piece of wood. Suddenly there was a loud crack. Using brute strength Serena had broken the furring strip right off of the gate. She waved her tail in a final gesture of feline dismissal and then easily walked through the opening that she had just created. She saw the problem, figured out a solution, and solved the problem. Cats are just not supposed to be that smart.

By now I had wasted most of an afternoon trying to protect a sofa that, upon reflection, I decided had seen better days anyway. Oh well, I could always get more furniture but Serena was irreplaceable. Oh, how I loved that cat.

Over the years I spoiled and pampered her. Her favorite special treats, possibly coupled with a genetic predisposition, allowed my furry friend to reach an ultimate weight of twenty pounds.

Eventually the day that I had been dreading arrived. Serena, now a geriatric grand dame of nineteen years, passed on. The Vet asked me what I wanted to do with the beloved remains. After some soul searching we opted to have our treasured pet cremated.

We hear a lot from the world of science about how people are composed mostly of water. Well, it's also true of animals. Some days after her passing, we received a package from the Vet containing Serena's ashes. The cardboard box was small. The canister inside was tiny. It's one thing to know a fact as an abstraction. It's vastly different to be confronted with it as a stark reality. Was this all that once was my twenty pound furry friend? Just these few ounces of minerals? The inescapable answer was a disheartening, "Yes."

Now what? I planned to have a private goodbye ceremony for Serena in the back yard. Just she and I for a final brief farewell. A shallow hole would serve to inter the diminutive remains. Oh, the best laid plans.

The problem was my young daughter. She was sweet, sensitive and impressionable. Up to this point, aside from an occasional departed goldfish, Serena was my daughter's first real experience with the loss of a loved one, and she adored Serena as much as I did. My main concern now was to spare my child's feelings as much as possible. Not wishing to traumatize my daughter unduly I had previously explained that our favorite cat was on her way to heaven and would soon be happily chasing angelic mice.

With the directness of the young my darling daughter inquired, "What did you do with Serena's body, Daddy, throw her away?"

Completely taken off guard, and without thinking, I replied, "Certainly not. Serena is in the basement. I was just going to have a goodbye service for her in the back yard."

My daughter perked up at this. "I want to say goodbye to her, too."

It hit me at that point that I had just made a very big mistake. How could I ever explain to this young child how her twenty pound pampered pet was now reduced to a few ounces of minerals in a tin container? She would never believe it was our cat. And if somehow I did manage to convince her, I knew that she'd be horrified at the information. What to do?

As an enlightened parent I opted for deception. I announced, "look, sweetheart, I first have to build a special box in order to give Serena a proper service."

"All right, Dad, I'll watch my cartoon show until you're ready."

Down I went to my basement workshop. There sat the tin with Serena's ashes on a shelf near my work bench. A wave of sorrow at the loss of my friend washed over me and I'm not ashamed to admit that there were even a few tears at this point, the first of many as I was about to discover.

So instead of a shallow grave for the tin of ashes which I could have dug with a teaspoon, I now began the task of building a coffin for Serena that would be large enough to accommodate the twenty pound pet that my daughter had cherished and remembered. Searching the basement I found some two by ten inch clear pine boards left over from a bookcase that I had made and set to work. As I carefully cut and joined the wood I reflected upon the wonderful years Serena and I had shared together and the tears began flowing. I even hand-lettered Serena's name in calligraphy on the lid of the cat coffin. I had to keep reminding myself that my labors would help to shield my sensitive daughter from any further pain after the loss of our treasured pet. By the time that I finished the job I was an emotional wreck.

I put the fuzzy blue blanket that Serena loved to sleep on into the box and gently placed the tin of ashes on top. Then I well and truly lost it. Deep wrenching sobs overtook me. I knew that I had loved our cat. I just didn't realize until that moment quite how much. Somehow I got the lid nailed down. Pulling myself together so that my daughter would not see and share my upset, I climbed the basement stairs and took Serena's coffin out to the back yard. I grabbed a shovel from the shed and began to dig a deep hole for Serena's final resting place. As I dug the tears began again.

Finally and mercifully, all was ready for the service. I clung to the thought that my main purpose was to spare my impressionable young child any upset or trauma. Collecting myself once more, I returned to the house. My daughter was still in the family room riveted to the television.

"Sweetheart," I announced, "I'm ready to begin Serena's service. Let's go out to the yard and say our final goodbyes."

"Okay, Dad," my sensitive child sweetly responded, "right after this cartoon show is over."

Stunned, I couldn't believe what I was hearing. I had turned myself emotionally inside out to spare this kid any unnecessary pain over the loss of our treasured friend and all she cared about was her stupid cartoon show?

I simply could not prolong the agony for myself one minute longer.

"Listen," I all but shouted, "I'm having the service right now. Come out to the yard if you want to."

Without any seeming concern my daughter turned back to the animated images chasing each other around the T.V. screen. "I'll be there in a minute."

I stormed out of the house and returned to the backyard. There, next to the three foot deep hole that I had dug at major emotional cost, lay the twenty pound cat sized coffin I had just constructed. As I filled the hole I lost it one last time as I said my final farewell. I replaced the shovel in the shed and returned to the house.

As I passed the family room I announced to my daughter, "Well, it's done. I said goodbye to Serena."

My daughter innocently turned to look back at me. "The show's over, Dad. Let's have the service now."

"Didn't you hear me? I told you it's done. The service for Serena is finished."

Then, my sweet, loving and sensitive child that I had taken such pains to shield from any hurt or emotional trauma looked up at me and asked, "Dad, can you dig her up and do it over?"

# Car Trouble

When we moved to our home on Long Island from an apartment in Brooklyn, New York, I began a daily commute each way of about thirty miles on the infamous Belt Parkway. For those of you fortunate enough to be unfamiliar with this exceedingly treacherous road the Belt Parkway, a.k.a. simply THE BELT, was, and in the opinion of many continues to be, the single worst road in America. Driving to work one morning I spotted a bumper sticker which read, "Pray for Me, I Drive the Belt Parkway." Rather than pray for just that one fellow I offered up a silent prayer for all of us forced to travel that hellish highway.

This misbegotten thoroughfare was originally designed to be a link between the permanent residences in Manhattan and Brooklyn, and the summer homes of the rich on Long Island. The designers, in their infinite wisdom, had failed to consider the possibility that Long Island would eventually become a gigantic suburban Mecca for those fleeing New York City. The consequence of such lack of foresight was now a huge volume of cars traveling each day on a highway totally ill equipped to handle them.

Your run of the mill aggressive New York driver pales by comparison when compared with the savage and death defying driving skills necessary to navigate the Belt Parkway. We daily commuters handled the challenge of The Belt by developing interesting and innovative strategies and techniques. For example, tailgating on The Belt was developed to the level of an art form.

NASCAR drivers use a technique called drafting. This is when one car rides close behind the bumper of the one ahead. The vehicle in front blocks the wind and virtually pulls the trailing car along in its wake. I'm convinced that this method of driving was not only developed but perfected on the Belt Parkway.

Most people understand that normally a distance of several car lengths between vehicles is a necessary safety margin at highway speeds. This understanding was totally ignored on The Belt. Any space greater than a single car length was instantly interpreted as a lucky break in the flow of traffic, just begging to be exploited. It was viewed by the other drivers simply as an opportunity to move up in the automotive pecking order. Any motorist foolish or inexperienced enough to allow any extra space was immediately confronted by other drivers racing to get ahead of their adversaries. Occasionally these would-be road warriors arrived at this targeted location at exactly the same moment. The resulting collision would then shut down The Belt for hours. Many a commuter who showed up late for work has used the universally accepted excuse, "Another pileup on The Belt."

Changing lanes was also an adventure. In a rational world a driver wishing to move from one lane to another naturally first signals his intention to do so. It would have been the height of folly to attempt this on The Belt where rush hour madness reigned supreme. To signal before changing lanes always encouraged the driver behind to speed up to prevent you from doing so. This resulted in what was known on The Belt as "A Near Miss." No one blamed him. We Belt commuters expected it. We understood that he was merely honing his necessary cutoff skills as we all were.

What we did to counter the cut off maneuver was to simply change lanes first and only signal once we had safely occupied the lane of our choosing. If in so doing we had cut off the car behind, so much the better. Each "Near Miss", and I had at least two a day, served to further sharpen our reflexes and allowed us to react to the unexpected with split second timing.

On The Belt the long list of traffic rules inscribed in the drivers' handbook were abandoned to be replaced by an all encompassing substitute. There was but one single and overriding concept that all travelers on The Belt followed to the letter: "It's Every Man and Woman for Themselves."

The posted fifty five mile per hour speed limit was taken by the drivers of The Belt as a rather bad joke the authorities had attempted to play on the clueless. Heaven help the unwary who wandered into the fast lane and was not traveling at least two or three light years over the speed limit. It was then considered the unspoken responsibility of the driver behind to move up and ride the bumper of this misguided slow poke so as to encourage him to get the heck out of the way. There was never any shortage of volunteers to provide this service for their fellow commuters.

Since virtually the entire Belt Parkway commuting public totally ignored the posted speed limit we were all fish in a barrel for the predatory but cheerful traffic cops that were an ever present threat. As the officer handed the hapless commuter a ticket requiring a hundred dollar or more fine, the thoughtful cop never forgot to wish him a nice day. Although the Mayor's office repeatedly denied it, the blizzards of tickets were written according to the monthly quota as set by The City.

As we drove up and down the length of The Belt, we long suffering commuters exchanged our own special salute with each other. This apparent gesture of greeting was known to New Yorkers as "Flipping the Bird." To the casual out of town observer, this ritual may have looked, at first glance, like we all belonged to some secret fraternity.

The Bird was easy to master. To signal other drivers using "The Bird" all that was needed was to hold up a single finger in their direction. This gesture of concern was designed to indicate to the recipient that, in the opinion of the flipper, additional driving lessons were necessary in order for the flippee to safely navigate The Belt in the future. It was customary for the flippee to answer with an enthusiastic flip of his own. Some recipients of The Bird were so grateful for the flipper's interest in their well being that they would speed up and race alongside the flipper's car offering many repeated flips of their own in gratitude.

The Belt was dotted all along its length with potholes of varying depths. These ranged from shallow depressions in the roadway to the giant vehicle mangling kind. The Department of Transportation workers had an interesting way of dealing with these menaces to navigation. They didn't look at filling the potholes as a job to be done or a problem to be solved. Sure the holes were filled but they were never permanently fixed. There was no intention or incentive to do so. Rather, these wily city workers viewed the potholes on The Belt as a kind of annuity which were there to provide them job security in perpetuity.

The D.O.T. workers were in no hurry to complete the work of actually filling them in either. They would set up their orange cones and block off either the east or west bound lanes of traffic. When one of these lanes was neatly immobilized they would begin their practiced ritual of shovel leaning. Several workers, and I use that term loosely, would gather around the hole and study the job while leaning heavily on their shovels. Why filling a simple hole required such intense scrutiny has always escaped me.

I don't know what they put into those holes but whatever it was it didn't last more than a single season. The stuff must have been porous because water would seep down and during the winter the ice that formed would expand. Then the pothole filling would just crumble away as the traffic pounded away at it in the spring. The holes filled in the summer would reappear after the winter like so many lethal spring flowers, but we never knew where until it was often too late.

Should any of us commuters happen to hit a pothole as we were engaged in flipping The Bird, tailgating, practicing the cut-off maneuver or any of the other essential death defying gyrations required of us on The Belt, The City had a unique way of dealing with any resulting damage to one's car. They actually had a statute that essentially indicated, "In order to make a claim against the city for any damage incurred from a pothole, the motorist first must alert New York City of the presence and location of the pothole, in writing, at least two weeks before hitting the offending crater." In other words, you were supposed to spot the pothole, note its exact location and notify the city in writing in advance. You would only then presumably be free to blithely drive into it, damage your car and make a claim against the city. Rather than waste all of that ink and paper The City could simply have mandated, "You can't ever win a claim and we will never pay you a dime if you try to do so." I just love politicians and the lawyers who serve them.

For the drivers of The Belt dealing with pot hole repair crews was bad enough, but any major construction on the Belt Parkway was an absolute nightmare. There were several overpasses that spanned the water and one unhappy day a D.O.T. road crew showed up to theoretically fix one of these. They blocked off one of the lanes with their official looking cones and set up their equipment. A D.O.T. lady wearing an orange vest and a bored expression had the sole job of standing on the roadway holding a red flag in one hand and a coffee cup in the other. I suppose she was there to make sure that we commuters slowed to a halt and not hit the other cup-wielding D.O.T workers. She never moved or even slightly waved her flag. To all intents and purposes she could have been a statue with one notable exception. If I were stalled at the overpass in question long enough I would see her occasionally take a sip of her coffee. This was the only sign of life that I ever detected. One day, as I had almost passed this site of indolence and sloth, I summoned up the nerve to yell out the window, "Get to work!" I then quickly sped away before any of the road crew could put down their cups and retaliate.

Traffic moved so slowly at this supposed repair site that if I dared, I could have reached out and patted the flag lady on the fanny. This job was so diligently implemented by these city workers that it took over two years to complete. The escalating cost in dollars was nothing when contrasted with the rise in blood pressure among the commuters. Once, when I was traveling through Wyoming, I saw a road crew laying a complete blacktop highway at about the same speed as one would unroll a carpet. I remember wondering at the time why the New York D.O.T. workers couldn't do that as well. Silly me.

Probably the greatest hazard on The Belt was from drivers who were not seasoned regular commuters. The Parkway was infamous for the traffic clipping along at breakneck speed and then suddenly, for no apparent reason, coming to a complete and sudden halt. A new car-eating pothole may have opened or a crash might have occurred up ahead. We never knew what to expect but we all had to be ready. Experienced commuters on The Belt were familiar with this phenomenon and never took their eyes off the road ahead even for a second. The inexperienced did so at their peril.

One time we were going to take my dad out to dinner for his birthday. He lived in Brooklyn and a trip down The Belt was unfortunately necessary. I wanted my wife and kids to travel together in our family car but my daughter insisted on riding with her boyfriend and followed behind us. The boyfriend was a safe driver but he was not a veteran of the dreaded Belt. So, while adjusting the radio, he briefly took his eyes off the road. In that moment he failed to see that the cars ahead had come to an unexpected stop. By the time he looked up he had only seconds to react. The first I knew of this was the sound of screeching brakes directly behind us. I saw him coming fast in my rear view mirror and shouted to my wife and son to brace themselves. The boyfriend was able to slow his vehicle somewhat but still hit us at about thirty five miles an hour.

I had a big heavy station wagon at the time and the poor kid had some little compact thing. My car suffered a bent rear bumper but the hood of the kid's vehicle folded like an accordion right up to the windshield. Fortunately, with the exception of some sheet metal, the only damage done was to the birthday party that never happened. Dad, who had stood impatiently waiting outside his apartment building for over two hours, was only slightly pacified when we told him about the accident. After establishing that everyone was all right, the boyfriend was torn between grief over his demolished car and embarrassment for running into us. As he was only a rookie of The Belt I reassured him that I bore him no ill will. Had he been a veteran, I no doubt would have felt differently.

I made my daily commute in what my children ultimately dubbed "The Boom Boom Car." This vehicle was so named because it had suffered several accidents, none of which I hasten to add, were my fault. The first collision the Boom Boom Car encountered resulted in a relatively minor crumpled fender so I opted to simply hammer it out myself until I could get to a body shop. The resulting repair wasn't beautiful but the car was drivable. It was an O.K. temporary fix.

I discovered a surprising thing during the next morning rush hour. The road warriors of The Belt seemed to interpret the damaged fender as a commentary on my driving skills and went out of their way to avoid me. The poorly repaired body work on my car was an excellent deterrent to their aggressive driving. This clearly was a very good thing and I filed this information away for future reference.

So, after each subsequent accident I decided to pocket the insurance money, rather than transfer the payment to some rip-off body shop. In almost all cases what was required was to simply bang out the offended sheet metal with my trusty hammer.

I have always maintained my automobiles to the highest safety standards and the Boom Boom Car was no exception. It had the best tires and all of its systems were flawlessly serviced. The other commuters had no way of knowing that mechanically it was in top shape. All they could see was the body. With each do-it-myself repair the car looked worse but my safety margin on The Belt got better. With every subsequent accident there was less incentive for me to professionally repair the damage. I eventually developed a kind of invisible buffer zone around my car as I traveled to work each day. I was enjoying the new found respect that I was getting on The Belt as the other madcap commuters rushed to get out of my way fearing no doubt that if they didn't their vehicles might otherwise suffer the same fate as mine had.

Just when I was really getting used to my exclusive status on the parkway my wife decided to give me her female point of view: "Would you please park that wreck down the street when you come home from work. I'm embarrassed for the neighbors to see it when you pull up in front of our house." Sometimes she just doesn't get what's truly important.

One of the most hated situations on The Belt was a rubbernecking delay because the havoc it caused was so unnecessary. There is an irrational feeling among experienced Belt drivers that all rubberneckers who seriously delay the commute should be hunted down and killed. I say irrational because every driver rubbernecks, but of course blames every other one for doing so. Once a guy who was illegally fishing on an overpass caught a very large fish and hung it on a railing by a heavy rope. The Belt came to a virtual halt as almost every single commuter had to slow down and get a look at the darn fish. That morning I was two hours late for work. With all of the police that patrolled The Belt you would think that at least one would have come along and made the guy remove that fish. Where is a cop when you need one? For all I knew one might have stopped and asked what kind of bait the fisherman was using.

One day as I was passing a newsstand on the way to my car, a headline on the front page of a local Brooklyn newspaper caught my eye. "City to install traffic lights on The Belt Parkway" stood out in bold type. I snatched up the paper and quickly scanned the article. The City planned to place traffic lights along the entire length of the Belt in order to reduce the large number of traffic accidents. I just couldn't believe it. The Belt was next to impossible to navigate as it was and now there were going to be stop lights. This was the height of insanity. Disgusted, I got into my car, threw the paper on the back seat and headed for the Hellish Parkway.

All the way home I was seething. "How am I ever going to get to work once they install those stupid lights?" I wondered.

"That's it, we're moving," I announced as I walked through the door.

"Why?" asked my wife. "What happened?"

I flung the paper down in front of her.

"Here, read it yourself," I exclaimed. "The fools running The City have finally gone totally crazy. There's no way we can stay here any longer. Getting to work is going to be just impossible."

When she finished reading the article she leafed through the newspaper for a few pages and then began to smile.

Seeing her grinning I demanded, my voice rising, "What's so funny? Don't you understand that we can't get to work once they install those lights?"

As her smile got bigger I got angrier.

"Will you please tell me what you find so funny about this situation?"

"Did you happen to notice the date of this paper?" she asked.

"I don't see what difference that makes."

"Well, look at it."

I snatched the paper out of her hand and glanced at the date. It was then that I understood what she found so amusing. The date was April first. The local Brooklyn newspaper had put out an April Fools' Day issue consisting entirely of untrue and ridiculous stories. The Belt was such a nightmare that I had easily accepted the traffic light story as factual. Greatly relieved, I had to smile to myself as I realized that the biggest fool on that April Fools' Day turned out to be me. However, believe it or not, a few years later when a developer built a shopping mall along a section of the Parkway, The City in its infinite wisdom, actually did install a stop light on The Belt at that location. So the April Fools' Day edition of the newspaper turned out to be somewhat prophetic after all.

Ultimately we moved away from New York and I got to bid a not so fond farewell to the dreaded Belt. Sometime later my son decided to drive back and visit friends in our old neighborhood. En route he became enmeshed in one of those infamous Belt Parkway traffic jams. He called me on his cell phone.

"Hey, Dad," he said, "I'm stuck in traffic on The Belt. The cars are not moving at all. This road is the absolute worst. How did you ever commute on it for all of those years?"

I answered, "Well, Son, I did it so that I could feed you and your sister."

With an outlook that only the young can afford he responded definitively, "Well, I sure wouldn't have done it!"

# Shark!

One day, as I was standing at the deli counter in the supermarket, I overheard two men talking. One of the men was very tan and fit. The other had grey hair and was kind of stooped over. The grey-haired man asked the tan guy, "Since you've retired so young what do you do every day?"

Tan Man smiled as he answered, "Well, I've never been married and I have no children. So, some days I play golf, some days I surf, and other days I just loaf around. I pretty much do whatever I feel like as the mood strikes me."

Grey Man seemed less than pleased with the answer as he no doubt contemplated his own very different situation. I must admit that I had a flash of envy myself as I listened to Tan Man describe his carefree life style. I reflected on the hard time our teen-aged son had given my wife and me while our kid was growing up.

I love being married and I'd kill for my children, but my son was, to put it kindly, a very difficult teenager, or so it seemed at the time. I suppose if I had compared notes with many parents of other teenagers I would have discovered that our kid was no worse than most and might even have been better than some. But if it's your own child, problem behavior gets magnified in your mind.

When my son was four years old a trip to a major toy store should have served as an early indication of the trouble that lay ahead. I blissfully entered the gigantic emporium of childhood dreams with my boy in tow. I had eagerly anticipated his joy and awe at being surrounded by such a wondrous environment. But as we walked down the first aisle he looked at the overflowing shelves and announced with disdain, "This is all girl stuff." Undaunted, I naively pressed on and led him down the next aisle. Once again he surveyed the multitude of children's delights with a jaundiced eye before announcing, "This is all baby stuff."

Then, with a chilling forecast of what might lie ahead for an unsuspecting parent such as myself, my sweet, innocent and delightful four year old demanded, "Where are the weapons?"

We returned home with "The Viking Battle Ax Set", complete with plastic broad sword and horned helmet. The kid insisted on wearing that helmet around the house for the next two weeks. I finally had to put the Vikings to rest when either he or one of his friends put a hole in one of my favorite paintings during a mock duel to the death. At least I hoped it was a mock duel. My son is now an adult and to this day insists that the offending swordsman wasn't him.

As a teenager our son was a heavy kid. He had gained the weight gradually over several years. Although he was an active boy playing roller and later ice hockey, fast food, soft drinks and high calorie snacks over time had piled on the pounds. My wife and I tried everything to get the kid in shape. We sent him to ice hockey camp in hopes that he would skate himself thin. Risking life and limb I did Father-Son karate with him in a vain attempt to try and slim the boy down. We even had a personal trainer come to the house. Nothing worked.

He wasn't really a bad kid; he just seemed to delight in creating havoc wherever he went. He was the class clown in every one of his subjects. Tormenting his teachers was one of his favorite activities. The turmoil that he generated seemed to be just for the entertainment value it provided him. Although he was very bright, his grades were suffering and his behavior was getting worse.

When my son was thirteen the family went on a vacation to Key West, Florida. We decided to go deep sea fishing and chartered a boat. Since we wanted to catch something big, the captain of the charter boat said that our best bet at that time of year would be to fish for sharks.

I told the captain that this was to be a catch and release trip and that we would not be keeping any of the sharks that we caught. I was very definite about this. The captain told us that in order to fish for sharks you had to use chum. This meant throwing out large chunks of fish overboard at regular intervals to attract the ravenous beasts. The captain explained that there would be a two hundred dollar additional charge for the chum. It was the first red flag. I suppose, because I was in vacation mode, I totally missed it.

It occurred to me later as we began fishing, chumming is just extra bait, isn't it? We were already paying an exorbitant amount of money for this trip to begin with. We should not have been required to pay this chum charge for more bait. "Chump charge" might be a better description, I thought. However, before we left the dock the captain had craftily asked for my credit card which he lost no time running through the little machine that he had on board. Once my plastic was swiped there was no turning back. Only when Captain Hook, a name which later popped into my head and seemed to fit, was satisfied that the boat and chum were paid for in advance did he fire up the engine. He took us a few miles offshore and put out several fishing lines. The first mate then started throwing out large chunks of fish which I calculated to be costing me about five dollars a chunk.

We didn't have long to wait as one of the baits was soon taken. The mate helped my son strap himself into the fighting chair and the battle was on. A black tip shark about six feet long launched itself out of the water in a series of spectacular jumps. Our son was thrilled at catching his first shark as he reeled in the fish which was carefully released at the boat.

Captain Hook told us that black tip sharks travel in large schools and it shouldn't be long before we hooked another one. It was to be my turn to catch the next one. In the following hour, chunk after chunk of football sized pieces of fish went over the side with no result. The captain was puzzled. "I don't understand it. We should have caught another black tip before now," he said.

Several additional hours passed and nothing happened. Finally, one of the rods bent double under the weight of a large fish. Even though I was supposed to be next up in the fighting chair an imploring look from my son was sufficient for me to relinquish my turn. I've always been a pushover for my kids.

As he leaned back on the heavy rod it was clear that the fish on the other end of the line was big, very big. With great excitement my kid began the fight. As my son tried to reel in the shark, Captain Hook began to try and reel us in.

"That's no black tip the kid has on. I think it's probably a big hammerhead. That's why we haven't been catching the smaller fish. That big one was eating all the bait and spooking the other sharks."

My son leaned back in the chair, every muscle straining. I had never seen him so focused before. After about an hour the shark was close enough to the boat so that we could see that it really was enormous. Captain Hook now began his sales pitch in earnest. "It's unheard of for a kid this young to bring in a fish of that size. He'll likely never catch anything this big again. You folks really should consider having this trophy mounted."

Although the Captain was speaking to us, he knew that my son was listening to every word as well. As our boy continued to fight the fish he gave us one of those pleading looks that every parent is familiar with. My wife and I went into conference at the bow of the boat.

"Do you have any idea how much it costs to mount a fish?" I asked her.

"Not really."

"Well, it's a small fortune. They charge by the size of the fish and this one's a giant. We really should not even consider it."

As my son reeled in the shark Captain Hook made a final effort to land us. "This is a once in a lifetime fish," he announced, as the hammerhead came alongside. We looked over the rail and gazed at a fish that truly was a monster. The captain estimated it to be nine feet long and about three hundred pounds.

"So what do you say folks? Do we give the kid the trophy of a lifetime or do we cut it loose?" asked Captain Hook.

And then I got what was ultimately to be a very expensive thought. Up to this point our kid had not accomplished very much in his young life. He was doing poorly in school and losing the battle of the bulge. Maybe, just maybe, I thought, if our son had a tangible symbol of at least one success, it just might carry over into other areas of his life.

A giant shark mounted on his wall that he had caught all by himself might be just what the kid needed to turn himself around, especially since it had taken an hour to fight and reel in. I knew it required tremendous concentration and perseverance to achieve this result.

"Do you really want it?" I asked my boy.

"Yes, Dad. I really, really do," was his immediate response.

I then turned to my wife. "What do you say, Honey?"

"You know more about these things. You decide."

I can only justify what I did next as what I thought might be an investment in my son's future.

"Okay. We'll keep the fish."

Captain Hook and his mate immediately sprang into action before we changed our minds. They got a heavy rope around the tail of the monster and, with great difficulty, hauled it on board. We now had a three hundred pound very unhappy hammerhead shark thrashing around on the deck. My family and I prudently retreated to the flying bridge out of harm's way, leaving the good captain and his mate to subdue our trophy.

Back at the dock a crowd gathered as my son's fish was hauled up for all to see. The kid was on cloud nine as he posed for many pictures with his trophy. Captain Hook told my boy that some of the pictures would be posted on the boat's web site. I've never seen my son so happy.

The captain took me aside and said, "You and your family should leave now."

Puzzled, I asked him why.

"Because you don't want your boy to see what we do to his fish next."

What the captain then told me was that they were going to cut the jaws out of the shark and send it off to the taxidermist. The rest of the shark would either be discarded or used as chum to catch the next beast. I couldn't repress the thought that the chum would also be put to good use to catch the next fisherman as well. Our three hundred pound shark would end up as forty pounds of fiberglass. The only thing left of the original fish would be the jaws.

This experience taught me that it is totally unnecessary for anyone to ever have a fish mounted. Many years ago taxidermists used to do what were called skin mounts. They would use the skin and as much of the original fish as possible. Today, none of the fish is used with the possible exception, as in our case, of the shark's jaws.

Modern taxidermists have molds for every kind and size of fish that swims. The correct way to deal with a fish mount is to first bring the fish alongside the boat. Next, measure the length and guesstimate its weight as best you can. Then carefully release the fish. Next, call the taxidermist and tell him what you caught. He will certainly have a mold to accommodate you.

In fact you don't even need to go fishing at all to get a fish mount. Just call and order one. While you're on the phone, ask about the cost, a small detail that we forgot in the excitement of the moment. Finally, as soon as you recover from the sticker shock, quickly hang up and forget the whole thing.

In our enthusiasm and excitement we had never discussed the cost of our fish mount with Captain Hook. Big mistake! As we were leaving the boat the captain, who already had my credit card numbers, informed me, "The taxidermist will charge the down payment on the fish to your card. You should get your finished mount in about two months."

I left the dock with mixed feelings. Our son was elated. My wife was hopeful that the success our kid just had with the shark would help turn things around for him. I was worried. The last time that I had made this large of a down payment on anything, a house was the product in question, not a fish. Since the total cost of the mount had not as yet been spelled out we had, in effect, thoughtlessly given a blank check to the taxidermist.

Just two months to the day a big truck delivered our trophy. Three large men unloaded a ten foot crate made of cardboard stapled over a framework of quarter inch thick wooden strips. Our three hundred pound shark, now reduced to forty pounds of painted fiberglass, was suspended inside. Once hung up in our son's room it took up almost the entire wall. It was truly an impressive sight. Our boy called all of his friends over to see his catch. Some of them doubted that he had actually landed such a monster. Their doubts were quickly dispelled when he showed them a tape of the entire event. I had thoughtfully filmed the whole adventure. In his social circle, our son became an instant hero of sorts. The total charge for the fish was less than a second mortgage but not by much. In fact, the cost was so great that my wife insisted the price we paid was on a need to know basis. And she was adamant that, outside of the two of us, no one ever needed to know. I had to agree.

A week later another bill arrived from the taxidermist. It was for three hundred and sixty five dollars. Since we had paid for the shark in full I called the taxidermist in a huff. "What's this new charge for?" I demanded. "I've already paid you a bundle for the shark."

"I'm sorry. I forgot to charge you for the crate."

"The crate!" I shouted into the phone. "You want three hundred sixty five dollars for a cardboard box?"

He answered simply, "That's right."

I suppose I could have fought this last indignity but we pay our bills, or at least we try to. As I sat down to write what I fervently hoped was the final check to the taxidermist, I thought of the shark as, "The Gift That Keeps on Taking."

The ten foot cardboard crate had been gathering dust since the shark arrived months earlier. It continued to be a point of contention between my wife and me. She wanted to throw it out and I wanted to keep it.

"What if we move? How will we transport the thing?" I pointed out.

"We'll worry about it then," she insisted. "It's taking up too much space in the garage. Get rid of it!"

So I reluctantly broke up three hundred and sixty five dollars worth of wood strips and cardboard and reclaimed the garage.

As for my son, did his behavior change? Did his schoolwork improve? Was he any less the class clown? Not the least little bit. From age thirteen to sixteen the kid went along pretty much as he had been, the giant shark on the wall not withstanding. The only change was that his weight continued to increase.

One day his very best friend decided to have a serious talk with him. The friend said, "Listen, you're a smart guy, the girls like you, it's the weight. Why don't you just lose the weight?"

Later that day, my son asked, "Dad, do you mind if I join a gym?"

"Mind?" I exclaimed. "That's wonderful!"

I couldn't believe the question. Over the years we had done everything we knew to get his weight down. I had suggested a gym membership several times to no avail. I wondered what had suddenly happened to change the kid's attitude.

Well, he joined the gym and put himself on a special diet. In a remarkably short time he slimmed down tremendously and changed his life. His school work improved and he stopped torturing his teachers. Everything for him and for us was better. The boy who wouldn't walk around the corner began jogging two miles home from his gym workout.

On one of these runs a car pulled up alongside him. Inside the car were three pretty teenage girls who shouted out to him, "Hi, Cutie!" Elated, he lost no time telling the family what had happened. I couldn't repress a twinge of envy. The last time a car pulled up next to me and the driver called out it was an elderly woman who wanted traffic directions.

"Why have things gotten so much better for you at school?" I asked. It turned out that, as my son explained, if you were the trouble making kid, the class clown, or the one that created all the turmoil, then you weren't the fat kid. My son's less than sterling behavior during his teenage years had been a cover up to mask his insecurity about being overweight. Now that weight was no longer an issue for him the kid blossomed. His last year and a half of high school was a dream. His teachers were all asking him for diet tips. At graduation the school staff, who I thought really disliked him, now hugged him with genuine affection. He proudly received his diploma and was accepted into several colleges.

After graduation I took my son aside and asked him, "So all those years that we spent so much time, money and aggravation trying to get you to change, all we had to do was to wait until you were ready?"

"Yes, Dad, that's all you had to do."

My wife and I were both thrilled at our son's transformation from terrible teen to dream child.

Some years later we were preparing to move to Florida. A representative of the moving company was taking inventory of our stuff when he saw the shark in my son's room.

"Nice mount," he said.

"Thank you," I responded with pride.

"That fish'll cost you a thousand dollars."

"What? How can that be?" I sputtered.

"Well," he said, whipping out a tape measure, "this critter measures nine feet two inches. It'll need at least a ten foot crate. Do you still have it?"

"No," I said with more than a slight degree of bitterness, "my wife made me throw it out."

"Too bad," he replied with an avaricious smile.

"I know what that crate should cost. I originally paid less than four hundred dollars for it. So where do you come up with a thousand bucks?"

"The price to build the box is only part of it," he explained. "That fish will take up ten feet of space that we can use to transport other stuff in. We need to get paid for the square footage we'd be losing in the truck."

"Well, forget it. That fish has cost me far too much already. In fact it's still eating me alive. Not too bad for a dead shark."

That night my wife and I discussed our options. "We are not paying another penny for that stupid hunk of fiberglass," I insisted.

"Maybe we could sell it to a seafood restaurant," she wondered.

Our son quickly nixed that idea. Then I got a thought. I wondered if the shark would fit into our S.U.V. We had to get the car to Florida anyway. This might be a way to transport both at the same time.

With the passenger seats folded flat, amazingly and thankfully, the shark did fit, but barely. It filled almost the entire car, leaving just enough room for the driver. My wife drove our Sharkmobile, as we called it, all the way to Florida with the hammerhead's gaping jaws smiling out through the windshield. She was, as you might imagine, the hit of the highway all along the way.

The shark now resides on a wall in our Florida home. We continue to be its reluctant custodians. Hopefully one day our son will be able to get permission from his wife to display it. In other words, we will probably be the keepers of the shark in perpetuity.

For those who choose not to heed this cautionary tale and insist on having a fish of their own mounted, don't forget to keep the crate

# The Pond

I've always wanted to live on the water but, like many of us, I could never afford it. Waterfront property, for me at the time, was completely out of the question. So it was with some interest that I watched a garden show on TV as a man created a small back yard water feature. The process looked pretty straightforward. It didn't even seem to be beyond my very limited construction skills. This was an all important consideration as I'm not the handiest guy on the block. I'm fond of saying that the only tool that my toolbox contains is a telephone. But the pond looked like a project that even I could handle. I reasoned that if I couldn't have waterfront property then a small water feature in the back yard was better than no water at all.

Not trusting my memory of the TV show, I went out and bought a book on the subject of pond construction. A quick scan of the pages confirmed that this should be a fun and easy project. The first thing that the book instructed you to do was to lay out the dimensions and shape of the pond with a garden hose or a piece of rope. I decided that my pond would be about six feet across and three feet deep. The dirt dug out to make the pond would be piled up to create a waterfall. I couldn't wait to get started. As instructed, I got out a length of rope and confidently went out to the backyard. This part I was sure I could handle. I arranged the rope into a shape that I thought would look pleasing. As I stood there I imagined how beautiful the finished result would be.

There was just one thing though. The second step in creating my water feature was to dig a big hole, a very big hole. It was a lot of dirt to move and on this particular day I just didn't feel like doing that much work.

So, I wound up my length of rope and went into the house for a cold drink. As each weekend passed I dutifully returned to the yard to decide on the pond shape of the week. As I coiled the rope into various configurations I visualized how relaxing it would be to sit by the pond, watch the fish and enjoy the sound of cool water splashing over the waterfall.

But, I couldn't shake a nagging fear that creating the pond couldn't be as easy as the book and the garden show made it out to be. I suppose for this reason, as well as being a card carrying member of the procrastinators union, all I ever got around to doing week after week was to go out to the yard and arrange my rope.

Then one day, as I was at my usual post designing the pond for the umpteenth time, my daughter's boyfriend appeared.

"You still playing with that rope?" he rudely inquired. "When are you going to start digging?" A nice boy but short on tact.

"I don't want to rush into anything," I weakly responded.

"Well," he said, flexing his oversized muscles, "I haven't been to the gym in a couple of days and I could use a work out. If you want, I'll dig that hole for you."

In a flash, moving faster than I had in years, I retrieved a shovel from the shed and handed it to him before he could change his mind. As he set to work, youthful muscles bulging, I went into the house and settled into my favorite chair for a nap. The thought of all that work the boyfriend was doing had suddenly made me tired. In a surprisingly short time I was awakened by a brawny hand on my shoulder. There stood the boyfriend, not even breathing hard.

"All done," he announced. "Ya wanna come out and see if it's all right?"

As I rounded the corner of the house, right where my perfect back yard lawn had been, I saw what looked for all the world like a medium sized bomb crater. But the kid was good. The hole was exactly six feet across and three feet deep with a hill of dirt piled next to it, just as requested.

"It's perfect!" I exclaimed.

"It wasn't that hard, I think I'll hit the gym." And off he went. Ah, youth.

I reluctantly put away my length of rope. After all, we had spent so much time together I had grown fond of it. Now that I had a bomb crater in the back yard there was no choice but to go ahead and attempt to actually create a pond. Following instructions from the book, I spent several hours carefully lining the hole with some old carpeting I had. This was to keep any sharp rocks from puncturing the rubber liner that was needed to keep the water from draining away. It wasn't that easy to cut and wrestle pieces of carpet into place but after several hours the job was done. I was sweaty and my back hurt but I had successfully completed the next step. I couldn't help congratulating myself on the way my project was shaping up.

My wife, being all too familiar with my lack of construction skills, had expressed skepticism about the project from the very start. Proving her wrong would be an added bonus when my pond was completed.

The book advised filling the hole with water as soon as possible to prevent the sides from falling in. So it was off to the pond store for the all important rubber liner. The store was an oversized pet shop and contained a virtual cornucopia of pond stuff. Most of it was a mystery to me but the nice man behind the counter was eager to help and offer advice.

"I'd like a pond liner, please," I announced with confidence.

"What size?"

I was ready for him. If there was one thing I knew after all that rope work it was the pond's dimensions. "The pond is exactly six by six feet and three feet deep," I responded confidently.

"You need a liner at least 12 by 12."

My confidence beginning to slip, I asked, "Why so big?"

"To allow for the depth and the rocks."

"Rocks? Why do I need rocks?"

He patiently replied, as if speaking to a child, "To hold the liner in place and give the pond a natural look. Otherwise you'll just have a hole in the ground with a rubber sheet full of water."

I hadn't yet gotten to the page in the book that mentioned rocks. Now that I thought about it, I seem to vaguely remember that there were rocks involved with the pond on the TV show.

"Okay. I'll take the 12 footer."

"How thick do you want it?"

"They come in thicknesses?"

"Sure. The thicker ones cost more but they last longer. The thinner ones develop leaks."

"Why hadn't the book mentioned this?" I wondered.

"Well, I certainly don't want leaks, I guess I'll take the thick one," I decided, my confidence returning.

"You want the one with the reinforced backing?" came the next inquiry.

"Huh?" was the best response I could muster. All I had come in for was a rubber sheet and here we were playing twenty questions. The man patiently explained that the reinforced rubber would not allow any sharp rocks to penetrate.

"Oh, I don't need that; I used carpeting like my book said. That's okay, isn't it?" I asked, suddenly concerned.

"Yes, but the reinforced stuff is better and eliminates one of the steps. It probably took you several hours to line the hole with carpet, didn't it?"

I weakly nodded as the ache in my back began to throb in agreement. "Well then, if there's nothing else, that will be three hundred and fifty dollars. Cash or charge?"

"Three hundred and fifty dollars for a rubber sheet?" I exclaimed.

"Yup, that's the price. As I told you, the thinner ones are cheaper but they develop leaks. Do you still want it?"

They say that ignorance is bliss. The thought of my wonderful pond leaking forced me to reach for my wallet. As I placed my credit card on the counter my blissful state had come to a crashing halt. It suddenly hit me that what neither the TV show nor the pond book ever discussed was the cost of the project. All I had been thinking about was the construction and esthetic concerns. If the rubber sheet was this expensive how much was the rest of the stuff that I needed going to cost?

As if reading my mind the storekeeper asked, "Are you planning to have a waterfall?"

"Of course," I responded a little testily, "what's a pond without a waterfall?"

"Well then, you'll need a liner for that as well. Oh, and do you have plastic tubing?" he slyly inquired.

Almost afraid to ask I inquired, "Why do I need plastic tubing?"

"For the pump that creates the waterfall and to connect to the filter that keeps the water clean. If you don't already have them, you'll be needing those items too."

I left the pond store in sticker shock, and eight hundred and fifty dollars lighter. As I struggled to stuff my new purchases into the trunk of my car I shuddered to think of what my wife's reaction would be to this expensive turn of events. I decided not to tell her about the escalating cost of my project until it was complete. I reasoned that once she saw how beautiful the pond was any monetary concerns would be of little consequence. And besides, maybe the worst was over? Hope springs eternal.

Back at home I laid out the rubber sheet and got ready to fit it into the hole. Before I could get started it suddenly began to rain. It came down in buckets. That night I didn't get very much sleep. A recurrent nightmare of mud sliding into my pond kept waking me up. Wasn't this whole pond experience supposed to be relaxing? That's what the book and the TV show had definitely promised: fun and relaxation. Well, I was having pond nightmares. I wondered when the fun was going to start. The only enjoyable part so far was when my daughter's boyfriend dug the hole.

The next day, after the rain had stopped, I nervously went out to the yard to inspect for any damage. There did not seem to be much. The waterfall hill was a little smaller now that some of the dirt had washed into the hole but the walls of the pond had thankfully held firm. A quick check of the bottom revealed about a foot of muddy water. Can't work in that. So, tying a rope onto the handle of a bucket, I began bailing. An hour later, muddy but unbowed, I returned to the house to let the sun do the necessary work of drying things out as I read up on rocks. Now that the salesman in the pond store had reminded me that I needed them I figured that I should at least skim the relevant rock chapter in the book.

Another day passed and I assessed that the excavation was dry enough to receive the all important rubber sheet. I had been really looking forward to this step as my carpet lined bomb crater would finally begin its transformation. My enthusiasm rapidly evaporated as the thicker rubber, which I became convinced the salesman had sold me out of some sadistic sense of humor, fought me as if it had a mind of its own. The pieces of carpet that I had so carefully arranged decided to slip out of place at critical moments. The thick rubber protested every attempted fold. I would have fared better had I tried to neatly arrange an angry twelve foot anaconda. After several hours of this rubber wrestling match, and many, many, bad words later, I finally triumphed over the rubber beast. I did not have time to savor my victory however, as it started to rain again. In fact, it rained for several days. This, as it turned out, was actually a good thing because it gave my back, which now felt like it might be broken, a chance to recover.

Eventually it stopped raining. I couldn't wait to get out to the yard. At first glance everything seemed all right. Because of the rain I had forgotten to fill the hole to prevent the walls collapsing and so I was relieved to see that the pond had kept its shape possibly because the storm had provided about two feet of rain water at the bottom of the hole. But, as I looked down, the water seemed to be moving. Were my eyes playing tricks? No, on closer examination, I saw to my horror that the water was indeed alive with mosquito larvae. Wrigglers they call them. And wriggle they did. There must have been hundreds of the little buggers. I was freaked. How was I going to deal with this turn of events?

Getting a grip on myself I remembered that mosquitoes multiply in still water. Once my waterfall was operating and my pond fish were on patrol there would be no problem. But now…what to do? The thought of bailing buckets full of creepy critters was icky and then I remembered how as a kid, I had siphoned water out of my old fish tank. Perfect! I would drain the little monsters out of the hole. This was accomplished by use of my garden hose. I then filled the empty hole to the top with fresh water and went off to inquire about rocks.

The man at the garden center had the same cheery demeanor as the salesman at the pond store. I wondered if this was because both were equally adept at spotting a sucker when they saw one. I quickly put this unhappy thought out of my head and turned to the topic at hand. Up to this point I had blissfully gone through life rarely if ever thinking about rocks. Oh yes, like all of us, I had thrown some as a kid, had skipped a stone or two across a lake and even once accidentally broken a window with one. But all in all, I had taken rocks completely for granted. That time was now passed.

To my way of thinking the cost of things seems to be dependent upon the category the item is in. For example, food is moderately expensive but when it becomes French food, it's off the charts. Rocks, it turned out, are not merely rocks, at least when they reside inside the gates of a garden center. Here they become different types, with different qualities and each with a different price tag. The garden center man walked me through his selection as if we were viewing a collection of fine art. In turn he extolled the virtues of mica, granite, quartz and fieldstone. He sang the raptures of slate and flagstone. It was a veritable symphony of rubble. It seemed that each and every type of rock had its own wondrous attributes with wondrous prices to match.

I finally settled on a type that I determined would not leave us destitute. The next decision was how many rocks? The man explained that a pond of the size that I contemplated would require at least a full pallet of stone. I gasped at the cost as I handed over my credit card. He then added insult to injury by telling me that the rocks would be delivered in a few days for an additional delivery charge of seventy-five dollars.

"But I only live a few blocks away," I weakly protested.

"I'm sorry but that's our policy."

I've always disliked the, "It's our policy," excuse for legalized theft. If it's their policy then presumably they could change it if they wanted to. On this particular day the man at the garden center was not in a policy changing mood. I was finding out the hard way that when it came to prices, the merchants connected to pond construction seemed to have the same view of the consumer as do French restaurateurs. As I drove away from the garden center I was thankful that my wife had not been present to witness the financial bloodletting.

Two days later a big truck pulled up to the house. There was not enough space for it to go around to the back yard, so the driver had to deposit the pallet on the driveway.

"How much do all these rocks weigh anyhow?" I couldn't help asking.

The driver casually answered as he drove away, "Oh, about 3,500 pounds."

I gazed at this small mountain occupying the middle of my driveway with more than a little concern. The rocks were various sized pieces all neatly stacked and held together with chicken wire. There would be no choice but to move each of them from the driveway to the pond site by hand. But thirty-five hundred pounds! My newly recovered back began to twinge just at the thought of moving all that weight. This was yet another thing that neither the book nor the TV show had mentioned. One of my failings is that I'm big on blaming others for my own shortcomings, and so I felt the beginnings of a grudge forming against the both the author of the pond book and the producers of the TV show.

At this point my wife, who was skeptical about this "easy do it yourself project" from the beginning, decided to make an appearance. She inquired about my timetable for the repair of our torn up back yard. Then, gazing at the newly acquired road block, she sweetly wondered when she might be able to park her car in our driveway again. As if I didn't have enough pressure… I patiently explained that I had fallen behind schedule due to all the rain. As for the obstructed driveway, I swore to her that I would move all thirty-five hundred pounds of stone the very next weekend. In response, she rolled her eyes as only she can and returned to the house.

The weekend arrived all too soon. I put on my stone moving hat and approached the expensive rock pile. I had with me my newly purchased wire cutter since the rocks were tightly bound together. A snip here, a snip there and soon… SPRANG! The neat pile of stone seemed to expand geometrically into an unruly mass as it was liberated from its wire corset. There now appeared to be a whole lot more rocks than moments before.

I thought briefly about buying a wheelbarrow but reasoned that the distance from the driveway to the pond site wasn't all that great. "Besides," I thought, "I've spent enough money to this point. I'll carry the rocks by hand. This, as it turned out, was not the best decision that I ever made. I picked up one of the smaller pieces. It was heavy but not too bad.

Two full days later all of the rocks were stacked near the pond and I was convinced that my back would never be the same. I hobbled into the house to inform my wife that I had kept my promise at great personal cost to myself. Although not as sympathetic as I might have liked, she at least managed to refrain from any "I told you so" remarks.

I now had to cover the rubber sheet with all of the rocks that I had so painstakingly moved. It took several days for my back to recover enough for me to even consider this next step in what I was now thinking of as my descent into Pond Hell.

As I stood by the hole deciding where each rock would be placed I noticed that the water was moving again. The creepy critters were back, only this time they had brought their friends.

There were more of them, lots more. Why had I not figured that the little buggers would return? Once again my thoughts turned to the rotten pond book which never once had even mentioned the possibility of a plague of mosquitoes. But there was no time for blame as I had to drain the pond anyway in order to place the stones at the bottom. So off I went to get my trusty garden hose siphon. I have no idea how many gallons of water a six by six by three foot pond contains but it took over an hour to empty it. As I watched the hole drain I wondered how much all this siphoning was adding to my water bill.

Well, finally I was ready for the fun part. Arranging the rocks would create the look I was after. I had barely begun when my wife called me into the house for an important phone call. It was from a neighbor of my mother in Florida who told me that Mom had taken ill and I needed to fly down as soon as possible. This family crisis suddenly changed everything. My free time had just evaporated and the pond would have to wait.

I now had serious matters to deal with and would probably be flying back and forth to Florida frequently for the foreseeable future. I had neither the time nor the enthusiasm to complete something as frivolous as a water feature. As I stood in the backyard contemplating what I had wrought to this point, I couldn't escape the thought that what I was seeing looked for all the world like a major war zone with a large kiddy pool in the middle of it. My pond zeal may have gone but I certainly couldn't leave the yard in its present condition.

I came up with an idea that I should have had in the first place. I reached for my favorite tool, the telephone. I would call the garden center and hire a professional to complete the job. That night I slept better than I had since starting the project.

But my joy was to be short lived. A day later the garden center man stood in my yard shaking his head in disapproval.

Alarmed, I asked "What's the matter?"

"I don't want the job," he snapped.

"But, but, why not?" I sputtered.

"You dug the hole in the wrong place. You have hedges right behind where your waterfall would go. Once the pond is operational you won't be able to trim your hedges. Besides, this set up is all wrong. I don't want the job," he repeated with finality.

"But, but," was again the best response I could muster before he interrupted.

Perhaps seeing my agitation or maybe dredging up what for him passed as a compassionate gesture, the garden center man turned to me and said, "Tell you what, I'll take back the rocks, no refund of course. I'll fill in the hole and put the sod back for four hundred dollars."

"I can't believe this is happening after I bought all this stuff," I protested again.

"Best I can do," he said as he started to walk away.

I weakly called after him, "But the book said it would be so easy."

Getting back in his car he unkindly observed, "You read too much," and he drove away.

Dumbfounded I stood there thinking, "Another four hundred dollars to be right back where I started in the first place? It just wasn't fair." But this whole pond thing now seemed frivolous anyway in light of my mom's sudden illness.

So an hour later I called the garden center and reluctantly told the man that he could take away the rocks and put my yard back together. He said that the earliest he could do the work was the following week. I agreed, hung up the phone and, with mixed feelings, deposited the treacherous pond book in the trash.

The next day a friend of mine, who was also one of my neighbors, happened to come by. He patiently listened to my tale of woe and then we walked out to the pond site. He studied the scene for a long moment.

"Don't let that garden center character fool you. You've done most of the hard work here already. Come to think of it my oldest son could finish this job for you. He's put in a bunch of ponds. He'll do it cheap, too. Let me call him."

Later that afternoon, a flicker of hope passed through my tormented brain as I stood with my friend's son in the midst of my torn up back yard. I anxiously watched as he surveyed the damage that I had created.

"Sure," he said, "this is no problem. I'll remove those hedges, run a new electric line for the pump and waterfall, and put in the right plants. When you get back from your trip all you'll have to do is add the fish."

I shook hands with him with a tremendous sense of relief. I must admit to a certain satisfaction as I called the garden center man and informed him that I would not need his services after all. Off I went to Florida.

After a couple of weeks doing what was necessary for Mother, her health had improved enough for me to return to New York. My wife called to tell me that the pond was finished. I could hardly wait to see it.

Arriving at home I rushed to the backyard and stood transfixed. The yard that I had left totally destroyed had been magically transformed into a true suburban oasis. Those troublesome shrubs had been removed as promised and replaced with low lying plants that beautifully complemented the pond. The rocks were artfully arranged to cover the rubber liner and formed a natural looking waterfall. There was even a small Japanese maple tree to complete the look of the Zen-like garden. An hour later the creator of this back yard miracle came over. He showed me how to turn on the waterfall with a flip of a switch on the newly installed electric line. We took pictures in front of the waterfall. I thanked him profusely for his wonderful work, paid him in full and he left.

Alone in the yard I just couldn't believe the transformation. This was better than anything I had hoped for or imagined. It was even better than a lot of the pictures in the pond book. After all the stress I had been under with Mom and my, "I almost did-it-myself project", I decided to sit by my new water feature and unwind. After all, that's what I wanted the pond for in the first place and I had certainly earned a break. The sight and sound of the water splashing down over the beautifully arranged stones was a treat to the eyes and the ears. I could feel the tension in my body melting away.

As I sat there enjoying the cascading water something began to seem amiss. Was it just my imagination or was the level in my beautiful pond dropping. "No, it can't be," I decided. "I must be imagining things." So many things had gone wrong I was becoming paranoid. "Get a grip on yourself," I thought. I took a deep breath and tried to relax. But, after several minutes staring at the water level, my worst fears were confirmed. There was no doubt. The pond was certainly lower than it had been before.

"Why is this happening? Is there a hole in the liner? No, it couldn't be that. Not with all the carpeting and the more expensive thick rubber that I had bought. I'd better check the liner at the falls," I thought. "Maybe it isn't positioned right?"

I picked up one of the waterfall rocks and was shocked to see bare earth. Where was the rubber liner? I picked up another rock only to discover still more dirt. In fact, the waterfall rocks were merely set directly into the soil. There was no rubber liner for the falls at all.

This clearly was the problem. As the water flowed down over the falls much of it was seeping into the hill. That's why the pond was losing water. If this situation was not immediately fixed all of the water in the pond would drain away and the whole mound of earth that comprised the waterfall would turn to mud and slide into the hole. I flipped the switch to turn off the falls and rushed to the phone to call my friend.

"Listen, your son made a huge mistake with my pond. I need him to come over right away and fix it. How could he forget to install the liner on the waterfall?" I demanded. "The whole thing is unusable now."

My friend then made a confession. "The truth is that my kid really is not an experienced pond builder. He only helped someone construct one a long time ago.

But the kid is really handy and I knew he could do it. Besides, I wanted to help you out and he needed the work. I'm sure that he can fix the problem. I'll send him right over." An hour later the itinerant pond builder stood in my yard. Strangely, he didn't seem all that concerned.

"Sorry that I forgot about the liner for the falls. But we can fix it with foam."

"Foam? What do you mean?"

"You know, that spray stuff that comes in a can. I'll just spray it around all the crevasses of the rocks and that'll seal up the leaks."

"But doesn't the foam come out a bright yellow? The pond is supposed to have a natural look. That's not going to work," I insisted.

"When the foam comes out of the can it's sticky. I'll just throw some gravel on it before it dries to create the natural look you want."

"The liner for the falls is still in my shed. I already paid for it. Why don't you just take the rocks off the dirt hill, lay down the rubber and do it right?"

He explained that moving and placing at least a thousand ponds of rocks for the waterfall had taken at least eight hours. Softy that I am, I didn't want the kid to have to move half a ton of rock to redo the falls, and so I reluctantly agreed to his plan. He said that he would fix everything the following day. Still somewhat skeptical, I told him not to do anything until I got home from work. He agreed.

The next afternoon I returned home and went out to the yard. What I saw stopped me cold. Each and every stone in the waterfall was surrounded by a bright yellow foam outline. The effect was as if some deranged teenager had vandalized the falls with three dimensional bright yellow graffiti. I stormed into the house. My first thought was to call my friend and inform him that his son needed major psychiatric help. Thinking better of ruining a long standing friendship, I got the wayward pond builder on the phone instead.

"I told you not to do anything until I got home!"

"I had some free time so I thought I would get an early start."

"But the waterfall is all yellow," I all but shouted. "What happened to the natural looking gravel that was supposed to cover up the foam?"

"I tried it but it wouldn't stick."

"So why did you continue and foam up the whole thing? I don't want a yellow waterfall!"

"I figured that if the gravel wouldn't stick you could just paint the foam grey and it would blend into the rocks."

"Paint the foam? I don't want painted foam!" I shouted into the phone. The prospect of painting the foam to match the rocks every year was not appealing in the least. I had enough to do. What was wrong with this kid?

After a long silence, the mad pond builder said, "All right, if you really feel that way I'll redo the falls with the liner like you want."

"When?" I demanded.

"Well, I learned so much doing your pond that I just got a job putting in a very large expensive water feature. I should be done with that work in about two weeks. I'm sorry, but I can't redo your waterfall any sooner."

"Two weeks! I can't live with yellow rocks for two weeks," I thought. "I'll just fix it myself. I'll take the falls apart, install the rubber liner and put the stones back. I don't need that kid. It was supposed to be my project anyway."

But first there was the problem of the yellow foam. It all had to be removed. I picked up a small rock from the falls and broke off a piece of the horrible stuff attached to it. The foam came away easily but what was this? Yellow residue still clung to the stone and discolored it. I tried to scrape the yellow stain off with little success. I went to the shed, got a wire brush and attacked the rock with a vengeance. After ten minutes of vigorous wire brushing and use of the garden hose the small stone was only partially clean.

I looked up at the rest of the rocks in the waterfall. Each and every one was surrounded by a generous amount of the awful yellow stuff. How would I ever deal with it all? Dejected, I went into the house to confer with my wife. She patiently listened to the latest chapter of my pond horror story.

Then, to my surprise and relief, she announced, "No problem, this weekend our family will just have a rock scraping and washing party." It never occurred to me to inflict my pond suffering on my wife and children and I said so. My wife had no such reservations. "We are a family, and we help each other," she said with finality.

Sometimes she surprises me but she always comes through. My children on the other hand, took the news of the coming weekend event as if we had planned to boil each of them in oil. But no amount of ranting, raving, pleading or begging would dissuade my wife from the task at hand. As a matter of fact she even got my daughter to get her boyfriend, the one with the muscles, to show up on rock washing day.

The weekend arrived and so did the assembled crew. My daughter set the tone for the day by announcing, "This whole thing is stupid."

I couldn't help but agree. It was stupid but, as my wife reminded us all, necessary. And so we began to take the falls apart. We had to wire brush and wash each and every stone. It took five of us all day with only a break for lunch. Finally we were done. There before us lay about a thousand pounds of almost clean rocks. As a relative of ours was fond of saying, the results were, "Close enough for government work."

The next day I got the rubber liner for the falls from the shed and carefully lay it down on the hill of earth. To position the rocks that would comprise the falls I would have to get into the pond. This meant that all the water would have to be drained out once again. I noticed that I needed to do this anyway since, without a waterfall to discourage them, the wrigglers were back in force. The water draining away down my driveway served to dampen my spirits, as I was reminded again of my escalating water bill.

The pond now empty I only slipped ten or twelve times on the wet rubber as I stood arranging the freshly scrubbed waterfall rocks. Eventually I was done; and I mean in every imaginable way. I refilled the pond with the garden hose and said a silent prayer. With my last ounce of energy I flipped the switch to turn on the waterfall. The water cascaded down on cue. So far so good. My gaze was riveted on the pond. After several minutes of intense observation I began to relax. The water level was holding. My falls liner was doing its job. The work was over!

Broken but unbowed, I struggled into the house and announced to my wife that my "I almost did-it-myself project" was finally complete. She came out and gave it her seal of approval.

For the next several days after work I went out to the yard and sat by the pond. On one particular afternoon I reviewed the comedy of errors that finally had led me to this point. I wondered if it had all been worth it. Before I could decide, a dragonfly landed on a cattail and a brightly colored pond fish came up to the surface to take a look at him.

My question had been answered.

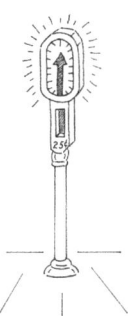

# The Man In The Green Suit

I hate driving in big cities. A root canal strikes me as a more pleasant way to spend an afternoon. But there came a time when I had no choice. It was necessary for me to drive into Manhattan and there was no way to avoid it. Several horrific traffic jams and a couple of near fender benders later, I eventually arrived at my destination. This was only half the battle. Now where to park? They say that New York has some of the most expensive real estate in the world. Space is at a premium. That might possibly explain why most of the parking lots require your first born as a parking fee.

I was seriously toying with the idea of returning home without completing my business when I chanced upon the Holy Grail. There, appearing in front of me like an oasis in an urban desert, was a vacant parking spot. I floored the car and narrowly beat out an elderly lady who mistakingly believed that her age and gender entitled her to special consideration. She should have known better. All's fair in love and an available city parking space. As I fed quarters into the meter the grey haired old woman pulled up and read me the riot act. Any twinge of guilt that I may have felt was quickly dispelled by words and gestures I didn't know grandmotherly types were even aware of.

A few hours later I had completed my business and returned to my car. As I slid behind the wheel I looked up and saw… a parking ticket tucked under the windshield wiper. Repeating some of the words I had learned earlier from the elderly woman I exited the car and ripped the ticket from the windshield. The fine was twenty-five dollars for an expired meter. I glanced over and sure enough the little red flag had popped up proclaiming that my time was up and making it easier for the dreaded meter maid to spot the offence. But what was this? There under the other windshield wiper was a second twenty-five dollar ticket for the same offense. The tickets were written five minutes apart by different official extortionists. I'm not a lawyer but I knew this couldn't be right. They can't give you two tickets for the same offense, not even in New York. But they had.

If you ask any city official if there is a ticket quota they will invariably deny it. They lie. As a matter of fact this is not just a problem in our major cities. The budget of every town and hamlet in our land is partially and in some cases even completely supported by traffic tickets. Municipalities use the pretext that they are merely upholding the law when in fact this blizzard of tickets is yet an additional tax levied on an innocent and unsuspecting populace merely for the privilege of driving.

Telemarketers for the state troopers used to call our home to solicit contributions. We did contribute for years but I finally put a stop to it. Now when the troopers call for contributions I say, "I'm sorry, we now give on the highway. Y'all have a nice day."

So, as a matter of principle I decided to contest the second ticket. Besides, I also wanted to save the extra twenty-five bucks. I pulled out of my fifty dollar parking space and began the perilous return trip home. Unfortunately, rush hour had started and the traffic was even more horrendous than earlier in the day. When I finally arrived at my door, I was completely spent. I did, however, manage to summon up enough righteous indignation to check off "Not Guilty" on the tickets and mail them away to that subsidiary arm of organized crime, the feared and despised Bureau of Motor Vehicles.

About ten days later I received a notice to report to the traffic court in downtown Brooklyn for my hearing. I arranged to take off from work and, with my evidence in hand, I prepared to strike a blow for all of my fellow down-trodden motorists.

For those of you who are unfamiliar with Brooklyn, the area around the court building is at least as congested as the one in Manhattan. In a spirit of generosity the city had provided a convenient adjacent parking lot which charged fifteen dollars to park for the day. I was here to fight one of the twenty-five dollar tickets but should I prevail in court, after deducting the parking fee, my saving would amount to only ten dollars. Oh, well, I was here already and there was a principle at stake. So I parked and entered the low rise crumbling stone building that was Traffic Court.

Once inside, I noticed that the edifice appeared even older on the inside than the outside. It was ancient and it smelled funny. Oddly for an office building, the floors were made of wood and they creaked. You would think, after collecting all of those parking fines they could have spruced the place up a bit.

As I approached the bank of elevators I noticed a portly man wearing a rumpled emerald green suit. People were showing him their tickets and he was giving them directions. When I walked up to him he glanced at my tickets and curtly said, "Second floor. Go to the end of the line." I tried to ask for further clarification, but he, slightly more curtly, repeated the same message. At this point it was clear that he had exhausted all the information that was his to share. So, with no other guidance or direction to go on, my fellow sufferers and I, clutching our tickets, filed into the elevator and rode in silence without any idea what awaited us.

The elevator creaked even louder than the wooden floors. Just as I started to become really concerned about the condition of the elevator's cables it wheezed to a halt. Exiting the elevator I found myself in a huge room the perimeter of which was lined with many closed doors. Each had a large white number on it. These, I was later to find out, were offices and hearing rooms where minor cases were heard. The real court rooms were on upper floors and were used to decide the fate of more serious offenders. The second floor it seemed was for parking tickets and the like.

The line that The Man in the Green Suit had mentioned stretched out before me. And stretched out, and stretched out, as far as the eye could see. I had to hold tightly to the principle that had brought me here as I made my way to the end of the absurdly long line. I noticed that many of the people had brought books, newspapers and even knitting to occupy their time while they were waiting. It was clear that these people had been here before. They knew the drill. I hadn't brought anything at all except for my two tickets. It suddenly occurred to me that it was just possible that my case would not be heard in a timely manner. Oh, how prophetic a thought that turned out to be.

More out of boredom than anything else I began to study my surroundings. I noticed that there were several women working on the floor who all seemed to be wearing outfits that resembled housecoats of varying colors and I could swear that they all were shod in what looked like bedroom slippers. The sole function of the housecoat ladies seemed to be to provide coffee to the faceless minions that no doubt were toiling away behind the closed doors that lined the room. Each woman carried either coffee cups or a coffee pot as they shuffled from one numbered room to another.

After waiting forty-five minutes I became aware that the line had not moved one single inch. Tiring of watching the coffee parade, I asked the fellow in front of me how long he had been waiting. "Over an hour," he said.

"Who told you to stand here?" I asked.

"The Man in the Green Suit," he replied.

"And has the line moved since you arrived?"

"Not at all," he answered, and returned to reading his newspaper. I asked him to hold my place as there seemed to be at least a hundred new people behind me at this point. He nodded and I began the long trek toward the front of the room. Eventually I reached my goal. The line of immobile people ended at an unoccupied and very battered looking wooden desk. I turned to the very first person standing there.

"How long have you been waiting here?"

The man lowered his newspaper and replied, "Over two hours."

"Where is the person who was at the desk?"

"There never has been anyone at this desk."

"Then why are you waiting here?"

"The Man in the Green Suit told me to."

Then I got mad. I looked around for someone, anyone who appeared to be in some position of authority. A man in shirt sleeves who had an official looking I.D. badge clipped to his belt started to walk by.

I blocked his path and confronted him, "I demand to know what's going on with the immoveable line and this unmanned desk!"

His expression changed from confusion to annoyance and finally to resignation when he realized that I was not going to go away. He haplessly looked around and then called over one of the housecoat ladies who was passing with yet another cup of steaming coffee. I briefly wondered how these people ever got to sleep after ingesting all this caffeine.

Mr. I.D. Badge turned to Housecoat Lady and said, "Sit at the desk."

Startled at this major shift in her job description, she bleated, "Why?"

"Give out numbers."

"But we never give out numbers," she protested.

The people in the front of the line, listening intently to this interchange, were beginning to grow restless. Mr. I.D. Badge, observing this, growled through clenched teeth, "Just give out numbers."

"But, but," the woman stuttered, "Where am I going to get numbers?"

"Just write them out."

"On what?" she lamely inquired.

In disgust, Mr. I.D. Badge began to rifle the drawers of the aged desk. As he opened each one he was progressively dismayed to find that every drawer was empty. Sweating now and down to his last drawer, he fearfully opened it and was greatly relieved to find a faded yellow pad with two crumpled pages left on it. There, lying next to it, was the badly chewed stub of a pencil.

Mr. I.D. Badge triumphantly handed the pencil to Housecoat Lady as if passing a baton in a relay race and announced, "Here, now give out numbers!"

Housecoat Lady once again resisted. "But, there's not enough paper to give out numbers to all of these people,"

Mr. I.D. Badge picked up the yellow pad, tore off the tiniest piece of paper and wrote the number one with the stub of the pencil. He handed the minute scrap to the first person standing in line who looked dubiously down at this prize.

"NOW," he all but roared at Housecoat Lady, "GIVE OUT NUMBERS!"

Galvanized into action, Housecoat Lady began feverishly tearing tiny bits of yellow paper and scribbling consecutive numbers on the pieces. She started to hand them out to the people standing in front of her desk.

Feeling as if I had just won some major battle, I triumphantly returned to my place toward the back of the line. After about another fifteen minutes we started to move. Not quickly. Not steadily. But, yes, we were undeniably moving. I couldn't help but think that I was the one that was responsible for breaking this log jam of humanity. I was the one that had compelled these minions of the city to do the job that we tax payers have reluctantly provided for them. I was sure it had to be the numbers that had gotten us finally moving.

Eventually I reached the head of the line and stood before the battered desk. There sat the same harried Housecoat Lady.

I noted that she had only a quarter sheet of yellow paper left. I thought, "I'm sure lucky to be getting my number. What are the other people behind me going to do when she runs out of paper? No matter. The numberless people will just have to figure something out for themselves." I was in survival mode.

By now an experienced number giver, Housecoat Lady deftly tore a minuscule piece off the yellow paper which at this point resembled a slice of cheese that had been nibbled on by a giant mouse. She wrote down a number on this tiny scrap and handed it to me. In a lifeless monotone she muttered, "Go on to room one."

Room one. Now we are getting somewhere. Tightly clutching my number lest it slip through my fingers leaving me numberless, I stepped out of line and proceeded past several offices and eventually stood before door number one. I had arrived. I was ready for my hearing. But alas, my joy was short lived. I entered to find long tables occupied by people filing out forms and yet another Housecoat Lady seated at an ancient desk that was, if possible, in worse condition than the previous one.

I walked up to her and handed her my scrap of yellow paper.

"What's this?"

"My number. They gave me this number and told me to come in here."

"I don't need it. We don't use numbers," she snapped, and handed it back to me. "Fill out these forms, make copies of your tickets and then go to room two."

Somewhat taken aback, I cleverly responded, "But…"

Looking past me she called out, "Next!"

Clearly no further conversation or guidance would be forthcoming from this cheery public servant. So I put the tiny piece of paper back in my pocket and, clutching the forms that she gave me, rejoined my fellow traffic offenders.

As to the number on the scrap of yellow paper, no one ever asked for it. In retrospect the numbers obviously had no purpose except to placate those in line as well as create the semblance that the people working at the traffic court were actually doing something besides occupying space and ingesting oceans of coffee. I kept it for the longest time as a kind of negative trophy of the whole experience.

My forms completed, I stopped by the desk and asked Housecoat Lady Number Two, "Where do I go to make copies of my tickets?"

Without looking up she snapped, "There's a line for copies out in the main room."

So, clutching my forms I left room one and reentered the fray. After stopping several people in varying degrees of upset I was eventually directed to the mass of humanity waiting for the copying machine. After fifteen minutes we had not moved at all. Oh great, another immoveable line. A nasty thought crossed my mind. I spoke to the woman ahead of me, who stopped her knitting long enough to agree to hold my place. When I got to the copy machine I saw something I had never seen or even heard of before. The body and cover of the copier had been modified to accept a large padlock. And there it was, locked up tight.

"Why is the machine locked?" I asked a man who stood at the head of the line reading a novel.

"They locked it when they went to lunch."

"How long ago was that?" I asked.

"Oh, I guess over an hour ago," he replied and went back to his reading.

I felt my blood pressure rising. Were all of these people sheep? Everyone seemed comfortable with each and every indignity heaped upon them. Well not me. Once again I scanned the room for someone in authority. No one in sight. I wasn't about to wait on a line for a locked copying machine.

I called out in a loud voice, "We need someone over here to unlock the copy machine."

No response.

So I called out even louder, "WE NEED SOMEBODY TO UNLOCK THE COPIER!"

A clone of the first I.D. Badge Man suddenly materialized at my elbow. "What seems to be the trouble here?" he demanded.

"I'll tell you what the trouble is," I parried. "How are we supposed to make the copies we need when you've locked the machine?"

"We lock it during lunch," he explained in a self satisfied tone.

"Well, I haven't had any lunch. And neither have any of these other people waiting here." I looked up at a large clock on the wall. It read ten minutes after two. Pointing to the time I snapped, "Lunch is over. Get somebody to unlock this machine and let's get this show on the road!"

And surprisingly, he did. He waved over yet another Housecoat Lady and whispered something in her ear. She quickly shuffled away spilling only a little coffee from the cup she was carrying. Two minutes later a balding paunchy civil servant grudgingly unlocked the all important copier.

Returning to my place behind the knitting lady I thought, "What did they do to keep the lines moving before I got here?"

As I ultimately stood before the newly liberated copier I was confronted by a hand lettered sign and read, "Quarters Only. Twenty-five cents for each copy." Here was yet another tax. A small one to be sure. But a tax none the less. Was there no end to the city's greed? Checking my pockets I found that I had no coins at all. I walked down the line like some kind of panhandler until I found a fellow sufferer who could change a dollar for me.

Now, tickets, forms and copies in hand I was free to scale the lofty heights leading to room number two. This, I was to discover, was the hearing room. I was almost home.

Expecting yet another line I was pleasantly surprised to find room number two populated by several desks manned by hearing officers. These were not judges but they did have the authority to determine the fate and fines of the various ticket holders. An unhappy looking citizen got up from one of the desks and a hearing officer waved me over.

I sat down and began to plead my case but the man stopped me. Glancing at my papers he said, "You got two tickets for the same offense."

"Yes, Sir," I responded.

"This one is void," he informed me, and scribbled something on one of my forms. "See the cashier and just pay twenty-five dollars for one."

Victory. Although I was vindicated why did I not feel satisfied? The endless lines I was forced to endure had resulted in this, a hearing taking almost no time at all. It seemed anticlimactic to me. Definitely not satisfying.

Before I could properly thank him he called out, "Next," and another ticket holder took my place at the desk.

Finding myself abruptly back in the main room I went in search of the cashier and found her at the end of yet another monstrously long line. While I waited my turn a very large fellow ahead of me decided to vent. He explained at length why he hated this place and everyone connected to it, and how he couldn't wait to pay his fine and get home. As the line moved slowly forward I listened sympathetically but noted that this was clearly a man on the edge. Considering his enormous size I was relieved that he wasn't angry at me.

After what seemed like an eternity the large man and I arrived at the cashier's window. The window was protected with iron bars and had a narrow slot through which to pass your papers and payment. The whole affair was constructed sort of like an oversized armored phone booth. The cashier looked for all the world like a woman in a tiny jail cell. "Next," she called out as the big man stepped up to the window and handed over his papers. The cashier glanced at them and then announced in a nasal monotone, "Two hundred and seventy-five dollars."

Grumbling, the large man reached for his check book. The nasal monotone from the cashier's booth announced, "Cash or certified checks only."

The man reacted as if he was suddenly punched in the stomach. "But," he said, "I didn't know how much the fine would be. I don't have that much cash with me." He took out a pen from his shirt pocket and began to write in his checkbook only to be brought up short again by the pitiless voice from the booth.

"Cash or certified checks only."

The man's eyes got wide. His jaw muscles tightened. His oversized body went totally rigid and a strange kind of growling sound came from somewhere deep within.

The cashier looked right past him to me and called out, "NEXT."

Suddenly, the large man abruptly snapped. He let out a primal bellow of rage and lunged forward. He reached through the bars of the cashier's window in an attempt to get at this, the most insensitive of civil servants.

The cashier backed up in her cage as far as she could and began to yell, "Security, Security." Several men in blue uniforms suddenly appeared. They were no doubt lurking nearby waiting for just such an eventuality. After a considerable struggle they began to drag the large man away.

The purpose of the bars on the cashier's booth now became apparent. The security of the structure was not to prevent a robbery of the city's cash receipts. The bars were there to prevent a homicide.

The guards continued to escort the unhinged man away, who at this point was muttering incoherently. Now, in addition to his traffic fine, he would no doubt be facing other charges. I reviewed the possibilities. The man who only wanted to pay up and go home to his family might now be charged with attempted murder, or assault on a civil servant, or something more serious in this environment, disrupting a coffee break. I reflected on how the system had successfully driven this unfortunate motorist completely insane.

My thoughts were interrupted as the cashier had managed to pull herself together and called to me, "Next." I stepped to the widow and pushed my papers through the slot, careful to keep my hands on my side of the bars lest she misinterpret my actions and call back the guards.

"Twenty-five dollars," she droned.

Unlike the unfortunate fellow before me, I was ready for her. I had brought cash. In fact I had enough to cover the fines for both tickets just in case I had not prevailed at my hearing. I counted out the money and she gave me a receipt. As I turned to go a wave of relief washed over me. No more lines to wait on.

I had survived my trip through the Traffic Court Twilight Zone and happily rode the creaky elevator back down to ground level. I walked past The Man in the Green Suit who was at his usual post guiding the unsuspecting to the infamous second floor line. I looked on with pity as the fresh meat innocently filed into the elevator.

I paid the fifteen dollar fee to reclaim my car from the parking lot, and began the long ride home. As I drove I reflected on the whole experience and the very small victory I had won. As weeks went by the pain of my traffic court afternoon began to fade.

Just about when I was feeling like my old self, I walked to where I had parked on a residential street to find yet another ticket on my windshield. I couldn't believe it. I read the nearby parking signs three times. This was definitely a legal spot. I wasn't at a parking meter. What statute could I have possibly violated? The ticket indicated that my offense was for an expired inspection sticker. The fine was thirty-five dollars. I studied the sticker on my windshield and saw that the inspection would not expire for at least a month. The ticket was wrong. Enraged I drove to the local precinct.

"I want to see the officer in charge," I demanded.

A sergeant, actually a rather pleasant guy, listened to my complaint and even came outside to look at the car. He checked the sticker and agreed, "You are absolutely right, Sir. Your sticker is valid. I'm sorry, the officer made a mistake."

"Great. So just tear up the ticket."

"I'm afraid that I can't do that. You see, once a ticket is written we are not allowed to alter it, but you can plead "Not Guilty". You'll be notified when to report for your hearing. Just go to the traffic court in downtown Brooklyn and you can easily clear up the mistake."

I drove away seething.

When I got home I sat down at my desk and examined the ticket again. I wondered if the cop that issued it had a reading problem. Maybe he hadn't reached his ticket quota for the week. Whatever the reason, I had a decision to make. There were two boxes you could check off. One said, "Guilty." The other, "Not Guilty." My inspection sticker clearly had not expired.

Once again I was confronted with a matter of principle. This time, a thirty-five dollar one. Always a person of deep convictions, I came to a reasoned, thoughtful decision. I grudgingly checked off the box marked, "Guilty" and wrote out a check to the Bureau of Motor Vehicles for thirty-five dollars.

Later that day I found myself standing in front of a mailbox, clutching the envelope containing the unfair ticket and my check. I was having last minute second thoughts. "I'm innocent," I thought. "I don't deserve this ticket. There's a moral principle at stake here, not to mention thirty-five dollars. I'll show them. I'll go home, tear up the check, change my plea to 'Not Guilty', and fight to prove my innocence."

Then, all at once, it fully dawned on me why the city has made a trip to traffic court only slightly less painful than a descent into the "seven levels of hell".

So, I dropped the envelope with my check into the mail slot and got on with my life.

# V.I.P.

There it innocently lay on the dining room table with the rest of the mail: the usual assortment of catalogues, bills and limited time offers for things we didn't need or want. I opened it to find that I had been pre-qualified and pre-approved for yet another credit card. Like all of us, it wasn't the first time I had received an envelope of this kind. But as it happened, the timing was such that I was receptive to its contents.

The issuing bank will not be named here to protect the guilty and to avoid my having to defend against any potential lawsuit. As I read the offer I discovered that I had been given the singular honor of being awarded not just silver, or even a gold card, but platinum no less.

I turned to my wife and said with pride, "You see, this is what you get when your credit rating is as good as ours."

The offer was for zero percent interest on all purchases for a year. Since my son was about to become a freshman at a private university I thought that an extra card at zero interest might come in handy. We could keep track of all of his college expenses on this one platinum card!

The enclosed documents gave me a choice. I could either fill out the form provided or call a toll free number. I like talking to a live person. I don't do well with forms. They make me sleepy and I always fill them out incorrectly. The female voice that answered the toll free number was cheerful and helpful. She took my information and told me that I should be receiving my new platinum credit card in seven to ten days. I asked her what amount of credit the card would provide.

"I'm sorry, sir," she sweetly replied. "That is another department and will depend upon your credit rating." This, the first small sign of trouble, went completely unnoticed by me.

"But, I've been pre-approved for a platinum card. Doesn't that mean that my credit rating is sterling?"

"Yes," she said, a little less sweetly, "I'm sure it does, sir, but as I've just explained to you that is not my department and you should be getting your card in seven to ten days. Is there anything else that I can help you with?"

Afraid to venture any further from her department I thanked her and hung up. Ten days later my card arrived. It was truly a thing of beauty. Blue, white and silver, with my name in embossed letters. Also printed on the card was the word platinum proclaiming to the entire world that I was a person of substance.

I called the activation number and was told by an automated, mechanical voice that I could now use the card and had a credit line of six thousand dollars. I must admit to a slight feeling of disappointment on hearing that I was only approved for six thousand. I wondered, was this all that platinum people get? I had to presume that the gold card people got less. I shuddered to think of what the silver card holders had to make do with. My questions remained unanswered as the mechanical voice droned on. The voice informed me that I could and should purchase a seemingly endless list of services designed to make my credit card at least as secure as the vaults of Fort Knox. It went on and on and instructed me to hit numbers on my phone to purchase each of these wonderful services. Reluctant to use up my allotment before visiting even a single store I abruptly hung up on the voice before I pressed any numbers accidentally. I know it was rude of me. I hoped the machine understood.

The next day I called the customer service department of Dell computers to break in my new credit card and get my son the all important college laptop. After approximately one hour on the phone and fifteen hundred dollars worth of obligatory computer stuff ordered, the service person asked, "Which credit card will you be using, sir?"

I proudly announced, "My new platinum credit card."

The service person asked for the credit card numbers, the expiration date and the three little numbers on the back of the card.

"How soon can we have the computer delivered?"

There was an uncomfortable silence before the Dell service person said, "I'm sorry, sir, but the charge has been declined."

"Declined! What do you mean declined?" I all but shouted into the phone. "This is a brand new card and I have six thousand dollars worth of credit on it."

"Well, they did allow the carrying case and the lower priced accessory items, but they declined the computer charge."

I told the Dell man that there must be a mistake. I would clear it up immediately and call him right back.

He said, "Let me give you my direct line and we can place the order when you call." I thanked him and hung up.

I turned over my brand new blue, white and silver credit card and gazed with reassurance at the twenty four hour customer service eight hundred number. As I confidently began to dial I was totally unaware that I had begun my descent down the credit card rabbit hole. As most of us know, when you call a credit card company a recorded voice asks you to punch in your card numbers and then asks an I.D. question so that the voice knows that you are really you. After that you get a live person to speak with. It seems a ritual that we must put up with in the twenty-first century. The live person who answered the phone sweetly asked how she could help me. I, just as sweetly, responded that she could rectify a terrible mistake and let me get back to shopping for my son's computer.

After accessing my account she said, "I'm sorry sir, but there was no mistake. The charge for the computer was denied."

"I know that. That's why I'm calling. But why was it denied?"

"Well, sir, there has been a lot of identity theft and you have a new card. Since we are not as yet familiar with your spending patterns we declined the larger amount. It's really for your own protection."

"Can you also tell me what good a computer carrying case is without a computer to put in it?" I sarcastically inquired.

She patiently answered, "I'm sorry for the inconvenience, sir. I have removed the block from your account and you should now be able to use your card without a problem."

And so, with my shiny new platinum card clutched firmly in hand, I called Dell again. I got the same pleasant fellow and told him that I had resolved the problem and was now ready to buy the computer. I asked him to please just put through the original order. He regretfully explained that once an order was declined it had to be cancelled and a new order written. Thirty minutes later, after painstakingly going over every single gig, bit and byte, once again he asked, "Will you be using the same credit card as before?"

"Of course. I just spoke with the company. The mistake is corrected."

I dutifully recited the credit card numbers, the expiration date and the three little numbers on the back of the card which for some reason are really important.

"Can we put a rush on the delivery of the computer?" I naively asked.

The long silence that followed was shattered when the man at Dell said, "It was declined again."

"What? That can't be!" I exclaimed.

"I'm sorry, sir. The card was very definitely declined."

"Look," I told him, "I'll get to the bottom of this and call you back."

"Very well, sir. I'll be waiting for your call." Was it my imagination or was there now a somewhat dubious tone in his voice?

I turned to see my wife standing in the doorway. She had overheard the tail end of the conversation and offered, "Why don't you just use our debit card to buy the computer? You should cut up that stupid credit card and throw it away."

"Absolutely not! This is a platinum card and I've got an hour and a half of my life already invested in it. There's a principle involved here and I'm not a quitter. Besides, there's a six thousand dollar credit line at stake at zero percent interest and I want it."

As she turned to leave the room she again tossed back at me with finality, "I still think you should throw it away."

Ignoring her advice I turned over the shiny plastic card and looked with new suspicion at the customer service number as I slowly began to dial the phone. I dutifully went through the ritual of answering all of the prompts before a robotic voice allowed me to speak with a real person.

"Yes, sir, may I help you?" said another female voice.

"You can let me buy the computer I've been trying to purchase for most of the afternoon," I responded with impatience.

"Your account shows the purchase has been declined."

"Yes, yes, I know it's declined. That's why I'm calling you for the second time today!" I angrily pointed out.

She sweetly informed me, in an all but mechanical tone, her company's position. "Sir, with the amount of identity theft lately and not knowing your spending patterns, the purchase was declined again for your own protection."

It was at this point that I must admit that I became slightly unhinged. I shouted into the phone, "WILL YOU PEOPLE STOP PROTECTING ME!"

The woman, now much less sweetly said, "There is no need for you to shout, sir. As I've already informed you…"

I couldn't bear to hear her repeat herself again so I shouted even louder, "I WANT TO SPEAK WITH YOUR

SUPERVISOR!" There was a loud click as she hung up on me. I stared at the phone in disbelief. Could customer service people just hang up on you? Didn't it violate some law, or a union requirement or something? Didn't customer service have to provide you with, well, customer service even if you were rude to them? Evidently not. I'm usually a very polite person but they had driven me to the point of rudeness. I didn't have her name so I couldn't even report her.

Just on the off chance that my blood pressure wasn't high enough at this point, my wife, who had heard me shouting, reentered the room. "I told you to throw that card away. It's no good. Get rid of it!"

"Nope, I'm on a mission," I stubbornly responded as I began dialing again. My wife rolled her eyes as only she can at moments like this, and then left me alone to press on.

I was quite an expert by now at running the numbers and answering the prompts and so got yet another customer service person in record time.

"Yes, sir," the voice said, "how may I help you?"

Collecting myself I responded, "I need to speak with a supervisor."

"Can't I be of service?"

Choking down my upset I calmly relied, "No, I really need to speak to a supervisor."

"Just a moment, sir, while I connect you."

After several clicks I heard a dial tone. I was cut off a second time. Was this a telephone glitch? Or possibly a cruel trick of fate. Were the customer service people conspiring against me? No way to tell. I doggedly dialed again.

This time, after going through the now all too familiar credit card gyrations I finally did get through to a supervisor. This lady was different. She patiently listened to my tale of woe and, after accessing my records, she exclaimed, "I've never seen this many notations on a new account before!" She was properly apologetic and said that she would try and make up for any inconvenience that I had experienced. In addition to removing any blocks she was going to put my account into a V.I.P. status. She informed me that I was now not only a platinum card holder but the V.I.P. category was one which very few card holders ever achieve. I thanked her profusely and told her that if there were more customer service people like her, the world would be a better place. She assured me that I was now free to shop to my heart's content with no further problems. I hung up totally elated.

I couldn't wait to share the great news with my bride about how I had persevered and finally solved the credit card situation. I walked into the kitchen and proudly announced, "You're looking at a V.I.P."

"A what?" she asked.

"A V.I.P. You know, a very important person."

As I explained to her what had just transpired her expression changed from confusion to pity and finally to a look bordering uncomfortably close to scorn.

"Throw it away. It's no good."

"Didn't you hear me? The supervisor put my account into a V.I.P. status."

But she pressed on. "Well, if you're going to go through the whole thing again with the Dell guy I would use our debit card just to be sure and not trust your V.I.P. position or whatever they said it is. I'm telling you that the card is no good. You've wasted more than enough time with it already. If you really insist on using the stupid thing then make store purchases with it that won't keep you on the phone hour after hour."

The confidence I had in my new status was shaken. My wife can do that to me because her instincts are usually very good. I contacted the man at Dell for the third time that day, assuring him that this time there would be absolutely no problem with payment. At the end of still another thirty minutes of computer stuff review the Dell man asked the now dreaded question. "Do you wish to use the same card for payment, sir?"

Did I detect a hesitant, even doubting tone in his voice this time? What to do? Trust my wife's instincts or my new V.I.P. status. I bravely decided to use my….. debit card and made the purchase.

No, I did not wimp out. Well, maybe just a little. My wife had a point. There were still a lot of things to buy my son for college. I would use the platinum card for those purchases. In fact, we had planned to buy a small refrigerator for his dorm room that very week.

A few days later we went to the local department store. A nice young salesman spent about twenty minutes with us extolling the virtues of various and sundry dorm room sized refrigerators. After writing up the order for the one we picked out he asked how I would like to pay for it.

With almost a flourish, I proudly whipped out my platinum credit card and handed it to the salesman. As he was writing up the order I casually announced that card has V.I.P. status. This proclamation got me a withering look from my wife. After running the card through his computer a puzzled look crossed his face.

"The purchase was declined. I'm also supposed to hold the card."

"What? That can't be right!"

"I'm sorry, that's the instruction," he insisted, pointing to the computer screen.

Sure enough, digitally emblazoned for all to see were the words, "Declined and Hold."

"But, but, I'm a V.I.P." I protested. "Call the customer service number on the card. They'll tell you I'm a V.I.P."

As the young man dialed the number I felt my blood pressure rising. After a few moments I heard him say into the phone, "Yes, I understand, 'Declined and Hold'."

"Give me that phone," I demanded as I all but wrenched the receiver out of his hand. "What happened to my V.I.P. status?" I shouted.

The soulless voice of credit card customer service replied, "That was good for only twenty four hours. Your status has expired, sir. You are no longer a V.I.P."

In shock, defeated, I weakly handed the phone back to the salesman. My wife paid for the refrigerator with our debit card. Possibly because he could see my agitation, the salesman, against his instructions, returned my new platinum credit card to me. On the way home from the store my wife mercifully refrained from giving me the "I told you so treatment" although I could feel it radiating from her.

A few days later a box arrived from Dell Computers. It contained a shiny new laptop computer, a bunch of accessories and a handsome carrying case. The next day another box arrived from Dell. This one came with the identical accessories and another computer carrying case. I had forgotten that the credit card from Hell had allowed these purchases and no others. Why this is so remains a mystery to this day as I made no further calls to my former friends at credit card customer service. As to the fate of the platinum card, well, I did finally throw it away. But not before I cut it up into the tiniest of little pieces.

There was one good thing though that came out of this entire experience. My wife never did say, "I told you so." In her eyes, at least, it seems that I'm still a V.I.P.

# Garage Sale

We had lived in our house for many years. There were two large walk-in attics, a two car garage that had never seen an automobile, plus an attached shed. The Chinese have a saying, "Something empty must be filled." And had we ever taken that saying to heart.

Every inch of space was crammed full of many years worth of living. In preparation for our retirement my wife decided to take stock of all the stuff that we had accumulated. Unfortunately she insisted that I accompany her. As soon as we walked into the first attic we immediately had a conflict. My wife picked up a sealed, unmarked carton and said, "Let's throw this out."

"What's in it?" I gently inquired.

"I don't know," was her answer, "but let's throw it out anyway."

"How can you throw away something when you don't even know what it is?"

She explained that she had read in a magazine that if you hadn't seen or used something for seven years or more then you didn't need it. The sealed carton in question had been in the attic since our move back from California over ten years before.

"Absolutely not," I held firm. "If you threw that box out without my knowing what was in it, I would never get another wink of sleep wondering what valuables we had disposed of."

She countered with an all inclusive wave of her hand and said, "It's probably just more junk like all the rest of this stuff."

It doesn't ever pay to argue with my wife, and so I thought the better approach was to take direct action. Before she could stop me I lunged for the carton and began to tear it open. She shot me a look as if to say, "You'd better find something good in there or you're dead meat!"

Lucky for me, I did.

Many years ago my wife's sister was in the Peace Corps in the Ivory Coast. She brought back hand-carved African masks for us that were not only artistic but were also very valuable. We had them on display for a long time but when we moved back from California we hadn't gotten around to putting them up again. Eventually we just forgot about them entirely. Since, on this rare occasion, I had been proven right, my wife grudgingly agreed to examine the contents of all of the boxes before deciding what to do with them.

"But," she declared, "we are going to give away or throw out what we don't need any more."

"What do you mean give away or throw out?" I exclaimed. "We paid a fortune for all this stuff over the years. Anything that you want to get rid of, we should sell."

"And just how are you going to do that?"

"Why, like everyone else. We'll have a garage sale," I announced.

"Oh, no. No garage sales."

"Why not? Everybody has them."

"Because, they're too much work and you don't make any money when you're all done. Plus, I don't want a bunch of weird strangers wandering all over our place. No, absolutely no garage sales."

"But," I brilliantly argued before she interrupted.

"I'm telling you, if you insist on having a garage sale then you handle it yourself."

"Fine," I said, not discouraged in the least. "All this stuff is worth real money and I intend to get it."

"We'll see." This I knew was the answer she always gave to the children when as far as she was concerned something was never going to happen.

Box after box, together we began our long trip down memory lane. To give my bride her due, most of what she helped me unearth might conceivably be classified by the uninformed as junk. But as I astutely pointed out to her, "One man's junk is another man's treasure."

She swiftly countered that this old saw was no doubt coined by men for men. "Women are under no such illusions. The female of the species can spot worthless trash from a mile away." And in her expert opinion, our family seemed to have cornered the market.

Undeterred, I pressed on with my plan. Like a real live Rumpelstiltskin, I intended to spin all of our straw into gold. The first obstacle I faced was the community that we lived in. Our town was an incorporated village, which meant that, in addition to having obscenely high taxes, we had to follow more rules than the I.R.S. tax code. One of these was that anyone who wished to hold a garage sale had to apply for a permit and, if the gods were kind, be granted a specific weekend to unload all of their unwanted stuff. This rule had a dual purpose. One was to limit the number of sales in town on any given weekend. The other was to extort a twenty five dollar fee from the hapless taxpayers of the community who were simply trying to make a little extra money. My wife observed that I had never held a garage sale before or even shopped at one. She predicted that I would be lucky to make back the permit fee.

I pointed out to her that less negativity would be greatly appreciated, along with a whole lot more help. And, to my surprise, I got it. She said that if I were really determined to have the sale, then she and the children would assist in preparing and setting things up; but she insisted that I would have to run it myself. On this last point she wouldn't budge. Not wanting to press my luck I agreed and so began my foray into the murky world of driveway merchandizing.

The following day, I stopped in at the town hall, filled out the permit form and grudgingly paid them their pound of flesh. The die was cast. No turning back now. When the permit arrived in the mail, I was elated. Our sale would be held in two weeks. But what was this? There was an alternate rain date. Rain? It never occurred to me that weather might be an issue. Oh well, I couldn't be concerned with that now. I had only two weeks to organize and figure the price of thirty years worth of accumulated stuff.

Returning home from the stationery store with a box of labels I excitedly set to work. It soon became clear that deciding on how much to charge for each and every item would be a more difficult task than it first appeared. As I lifted each forgotten heirloom from its cardboard resting place I tried to remember how much we had originally paid for it in order to figure a fair asking price.

I had hardly made a dent in this process when my wife pointed out that my approach was totally and completely wrong.

"I thought that you were going to be more supportive."

"I am. If you want to have a prayer of a chance of selling anything then you have to understand the mindset of the garage sale shopper."

"And what, Oh Guru of Marketing, might be their mindset?" I inquired.

"Anyone who goes to a garage sale expects to get things for next to nothing. The price they are willing to pay has little to do with the original cost of the item," she informed me.

"And how did you come by this vital piece of information?"

"Most of my girl friends go to these things, and we talk. The prices that I see here on the stuff you've already labeled are much, much too high."

"But if I price everything at next to nothing what's the point of having the sale at all?"

With a self satisfied smile, she looked at me and said, "Precisely." And she walked away.

I hate it when she does that. She leaves no room for debate or rebuttal. But, in thinking about it, I had to admit that my total experience with garage sales was, in fact, nil. I wondered if she could she be right about my prices. They seemed more than fair to my way of thinking, but on the off chance that my wife was not just having sport with me, I tore off the labels and started over. But, I resolved that there was no way I was going to sell everything at give away prices. However, now that I had received this new insight into the narrow mind of the average garage sale shopper, I did reduce the prices below what I originally thought they should be.

The next step was to place an enticing add in the paper. I agonized over each and every word in an attempt to pull in the largest crowd of eager bargain hunters ever assembled on one driveway. This task presumably accomplished, I got back to the all important work of determining prices and affixing labels.

Two weeks went by surprisingly fast. To add to my stress level, the day before the sale the weather man predicted a thirty percent chance of rain. This I quickly dismissed as an actual prediction of a seventy percent chance of sun.

The following morning the family was up bright and early. The sale was to begin at nine a.m. and we had a lot of merchandise to display. The larger, more expensive items all had price tags. We set up long tables the length of the driveway, each with different signs. One read, "Everything on this table: five dollars." There was also a one dollar table and even a fifty cent table which I grudgingly allowed. The tables with signs would accommodate the things that I had not gotten around to labeling. My son and daughter got into the swing and added loads of items that they each wanted to get rid of.

Stuffed animals were always my daughter's favorite things. But my kid, like her mother, had expensive tastes. It seemed that my daughter was never interested in the small five dollar stuffed animal on the bottom shelf in the store. No, it was always the large expensive, fuzzy wuzzy on the top shelf that she wanted. Naturally, I rarely deprived my first born the plush playmate of her choosing. My daughter had loved and cherished each and every one of them. She reluctantly agreed to part with a large portion of her collection but was still young enough to hold back a small army of her favorite critters. The end result of all that parental devotion was now displayed for all to see, like a huge multicolored furry mountain, on a blanket on my front lawn.

When we were finished setting up there was barely room to walk as the driveway was almost completely covered with the newly cast off goods of years gone by. The garage was also jammed to the rafters.

As our family stood there my son turned to me and asked, "Hey, Dad, how did you ever accumulate so much stuff anyway?"

Wondering the same thing myself, the best answer that I could come up with was, "Well my son, I suppose that it just kind of happens as we go through life."

Seemingly satisfied, my boy asked if he could go to a friend's house.

"Don't you want to stay and help me with the sale?" I asked.

"Not really, Dad."

One thing about kids is that they are brutally honest. I gave him permission to go and watched him ride away on his bike. My wife then reminded me that our daughter had a dance class that morning which they had almost forgotten about and they would be back several hours later. Far be it from me to interfere with my child's cultural activity, so I said, "Fine." They both wished me luck and off they went.

My wife keeps her promises. I was alone. I would get no help from her with the running of the sale. "Let them go. I don't need anyone's help," I thought. "How hard can a garage sale be?"

I took the time to walk the driveway for a final check before the expected legions of customers arrived. Something on one of the tables caught my eye.

"What is this? No, it can't be!" But it was. Prominently displayed on the fifty cent table was the piggy bank that we had given my daughter years before. It held sentimental value for me but obviously not for her. As I picked it up it felt strangely heavy. I gave it a shake only to discover that the bank was half full of money. Now this was a bargain any shopper could appreciate. A bank half full of money for only fifty cents. It occurred to me that perhaps my daughter and I should have a talk about the value of things after the sale.

Piggy now safely deposited in the house I returned to the tables and was annoyed to discover that my wife had taken the liberty of offering some of my personal stuff for sale without asking me. In the past, these items had come under her heading of, "What do you need all this junk for?" So, after hurriedly rescuing my fake prehistoric giant shark tooth and several of my other treasures from the dollar table I felt almost ready to face the public.

"What is needed now," I thought, "is a cup of very strong coffee."

Standing in the kitchen, I had barely put the steaming cup to my lips when our dog started to bark furiously. Looking out the window I saw an elderly woman in a loud flower print dress shuffling down the driveway. I glanced at the clock and noticed that it was eight thirty and the sale was supposed to start at nine. What my wife had failed to warn me about was that experienced garage sale shoppers often show up early to get the best buys.

Quieting the dog, I went outside still clutching my coffee like a security blanket. "We're not open until nine," I gently told the woman. I don't know if she was hard of hearing or perhaps she simply didn't care. I suspect the latter.

Ignoring me, she picked up a large straw basket and asked, "How much is this?"

Deciding not to lose my first customer of the day, after all, the poor old thing had probably traveled a great distance to get here, I said, "It should be labeled."

She examined it and, with an annoyed tone in her voice, snapped, "Well, it's not."

This oversight was a problem. Since I hadn't previously determined the value of the basket I now had to do it on the fly. It was large and nicely made so I figured that five dollars would be a fair price.

"That's five dollars, Dear", I announced in my best salesman like manner.

She abruptly dropped the basket as if the handle was on fire. She then turned to me with a sour face as if I had just said an obscene word and actually snarled, "You have some nerve charging five dollars for this." Then she turned and shuffled away.

I felt the beginning of a tension headache developing. Stress does that to me and I was suddenly feeling stressed. This, I astutely decided, was not a good beginning. I took a sip of my formerly steaming coffee to discover it was now barely warm in the cup. I reentered the house and had just sat down at the kitchen table when the dog started up again. I looked out the window and couldn't believe what I was seeing. Coming down the driveway was a virtual clone of the first woman. She was of a similar age and also wore a flowered dress only of a slightly different color.

Another glace at the clock told me that it was still fifteen minutes before my sale was officially scheduled to start. No matter, I went out to greet my second potential customer of the day.

As she approached I could not help but marvel at her similarity to the previous woman. "Maybe they shop at the same garage sales," I thought. She even had the identical shuffling walk. This thought was replaced with one of apprehension when she stopped at the straw basket the other lady had dropped like a hot potato.

"Feel free to look around, we have plenty of nice things," I said in an attempt to move her further down the driveway.

Undeterred, she picked up the very same basket, examined it briefly and asked me that dreaded question, "How much is this?"

Quickly deciding that I hadn't done too well at the five dollar level I confidently announced, "That basket is three dollars, Dear."

Her reaction was nothing short of shocking. It was like a bad dream. She practically flung the basket down as if she had been scalded then turned to me in a rage. "How dare you charge three dollars for this," she demanded. Then she turned on her heel and began to shuffle away.

I hated to admit it but I was beginning to think that my wife may have been right. Garage sale shoppers, it seemed, expected the items to be on sale for practically nothing. The sharp pain between my eyes told me that my tension headache had now fully arrived. This was not the way my sale was supposed to go. I had to do something.

So, I called to the woman, "Lady, make me an offer."

Without turning around, she flipped up the back of her hand in a sign of total dismissal and called over her shoulder, "Now it's too late!" And off she shuffled, presumably to another sale with lower prices.

I stood there stunned. I looked up and down the driveway at all of our stuff on display. Was this the way the rest of the day was going to be? No, I concluded, things can only get better from here. Without realizing it I was still clutching my cup. I took a sip of my coffee. It was ice cold. I hoped the temperature was not an omen of things to come. I braced myself and prepared to meet the crowd of eager shoppers that no doubt would be arriving momentarily.

My next customer was a little kid of about six or seven who went right to the area where all the toys were. My sale was looking up. This I could handle. Kid wants a toy; mom or dad buys kid a toy. Piece of cake. But where were mom or dad? The boy had come up the driveway with nobody behind him.

"Where are your parents, sonny," I asked.

"Oh, they're across the street at Grandma's." Picking up a toy race car he asked, "Can I have this please?" Hey, this wasn't a customer at all. This kid was the grandchild of one of my neighbors.

"Sure, kid, take it." And off he ran with his prize.

So far this morning I had given one thing away and acquired a splitting headache. Not the most auspicious start for my get rich quick scheme. I decided to retreat to the house for a couple of aspirins. Once outside again I discovered the boy was back, only this time he had brought his younger sister. After some tough negotiations with the children, I was one dump truck and one life sized doll lighter, with not a nickel yet to show for it. Score so far: kids, three; garage sale guy, nothing. My head was throbbing. How long did it take for aspirin to work anyway?

Five minutes later he was back again but this time the kid had gone too far. Picking up a battery powered walking, talking plastic robot he again asked, "Can I have this please?" Didn't this child know how to say anything else?

"No," I answered, probably a little too loudly as he jumped back in fright. "If you really want it, go and ask your mother to give you five dollars and then you can have it." Like a flash he was gone.

Was I stealing candy from a baby? Not at all. I had already given the kids three toys on the cuff. That electric robot, which worked perfectly, originally must have cost me thirty dollars or more. Five dollars was a definite bargain. In a few minutes he was walking up the driveway and in his hand the charming child was grasping a crisp five dollar bill. A minute later the deal was done. I had my first sale of the day and he had the toy of his dreams.

"Enjoy it, sonny," I called after him as he crossed the street to his grandmother's house. "Well, business is looking up," I thought. My elation was to be short lived.

A few minutes later my neighbor, the kids' grandmother, came stomping up the driveway. I could tell by her purple complexion and the veins standing out in her neck that she wasn't happy. She always was a little flaky but I couldn't imagine what had set her off this time.

"Just what do you mean asking my grandson for five dollars?" she demanded.

Before I could explain the free toys and the cost of the robot she went on to berate me for cheating a little kid and demanded the money back. She snatched the five dollar bill from my hand and stalked back across the street. When I finally recovered from the shock of her verbal onslaught I realized that she had not returned my thirty dollar robot! In fact, I never saw it or her again as she moved soon after.

I stood there wondering, "Am I the only sane person left on the planet? No," I concluded, "I am just as crazy as the rest for deciding to have a garage sale in the first place."

My next customer who arrived at bargain central was a middle aged man who, at first glance, appeared to be normal. We stood talking for a while and he really seemed like an agreeable sort. He shared some things about himself and I told him about our upcoming retirement. After exchanging a few more pleasantries he began to browse around. Picking up an item from the fifty cent table he approached me and said, "I'll take this."

"That'll be fifty cents," I told him.

"I'll give you a quarter for it."

Somewhat taken aback I responded, "You don't understand, all these things are marked way down from their original price. Fifty cents is a good deal for that item."

He observed, "You never held a garage sale before, have you?"

"And just how would you know that?"

"Because, if you had, you would know to price things higher than you want so as to leave room for people to bargain. Nobody pays asking price at garage sales. So, will you take a quarter for this?"

Indignant, I snapped, "Absolutely not! What can you buy for a quarter today?"

The man apparently was laboring under the delusion that he had some supernatural ability as he looked me in the eye and said, "I was going to wish you good luck in your retirement but now I'm not!" The guy put the item back on the fifty cent table and walked away. With this last encounter I was convinced that somebody must have put something in the water that had overnight driven everybody nuts.

Just when I was ready to give up all hope more people started to arrive. Over the next few hours I even made some sales. They were not big sales but there was a fair amount of volume and I was at last beginning to move some of the things that were on display. These people were not even particularly odd. My headache began to subside and I concluded that the crazies must show up just at the beginning of garage sales.

Then my wife and daughter came home. "So, tell me, how's it going?" asked my bride.

"Well, it was pretty rocky this morning but things have settled down and our stuff is beginning to move fairly well."

Just then a man approached holding a commercial paint sprayer which I had never used. He asked me the price in broken English and I pointed out the label which read twenty dollars. My wife, who was standing next to me, rolled her eyes and clicked her tongue in a dual gesture of disapproval and disbelief. The man turned away to his friend and they began to talk in a foreign language.

Through clenched teeth I said to my wife, "What's with the eye rolling routine? What are you doing, trying to kill the sale? You should be helping me."

She came right back with, "How can you ask twenty dollars for that sprayer? You'll never get rid of all this stuff at those prices."

Just then the man turned back to me and handed over a twenty dollar bill. As he walked away I pocketed the money with a flourish and a smile.

"Don't be so smug," my wife said, "That time you just got lucky."

Our debate was interrupted by a brand new bright pink Cadillac convertible that pulled up in front of our house. The driver of the Cadillac was a beautiful blonde woman who appeared to be in her thirties. Seated next to her wearing a pink dress that was almost the same shade as the car was an adorable equally blonde five year old girl. The total effect was directly out of Hollywood central casting. As the pair exited the car the little girl practically dove into the small mountain of stuffed animals. After rooting around for a few minutes she emerged with her arms loaded. As the pair approached I began to see pink dollar signs. The mother asked, "How much for all of these?"

I recognized one of the large stuffed bunnies as a very expensive import which had previously cost me a bundle. Before I could examine the other critters more closely to estimate their true value my wife piped up, "Oh, whatever you want. How about two dollars?"

As the woman opened her purse I pulled my wife aside and hissed, "Two dollars? Are you crazy? Do you know what the armload the kid is holding originally cost us? I even remember that big rabbit was an import from Belgium."

"It doesn't matter. Nobody wants used stuffed animals."

"Well, she does," I adroitly pointed out.

We were interrupted as the woman asked, "Can you change this?" In her hand she held out a hundred dollar bill. I had gone to the bank the day before to get change in anticipation of a big turnout. Now here I was counting out ninety eight dollars for a two dollar sale. As the woman loaded the plush menagerie into the back seat of the convertible her little girl sat cuddling with the expensive Belgium bunny.

As the happy pair drove away I turned to my wife. "Just tell me one thing. Why did you never do that for our kid?"

Knowing full well what I meant my wife innocently asked anyway, "Do what?"

Exasperated, I said, "You know, do what that woman just did. If you had gone to garage sales for stuffed animals for our child we could have saved a fortune over the years."

"Oh, I would never buy a used plush toy for our daughter," came the response. "Who knows where they've been?"

"Well, your attitude is exactly why that lady is driving a pink Caddy convertible and we're not!"

With that, my wife turned away and went into the house to make lunch for our daughter leaving me to reflect on our misspent fuzzy wuzzy past.

I knew that I could have gotten more than two bucks out of the Pink Cadillac Lady but the truth was I knew my wife also was right on several counts. Not that I would give her the satisfaction. Neither she nor I would ever have considered used stuffed animals for our kid because of possible germs. Also, once a stuffed animal becomes second hand it loses virtually all of its value no matter how much it had originally cost. I had often referred to our vast collection as the most expensive kind of attic insulation money could buy.

Oh well, on the bright side it had turned out to be a sunny day with no rain in sight.

The agitated man who showed up next shocked me completely out of my fuzzy funk. "See anything you like?" I asked as he walked up to me.

"No. I just came here to make sure that you were really having a garage sale at this address."

Puzzled I asked, "What do you mean?"

He explained that he lived in the next town over on a street with the same name as ours and the same house number. I knew the place. We had gotten their pizza deliveries on several occasions. The man explained that he had been taking a shower when he heard his front door slam. Wearing only a towel he went downstairs to find a strange couple standing in his living room.

"Who are you people?" he demanded.

"We're here for the garage sale that was advertised in the paper."

He told these two rocket scientists that they were at the right address but in the wrong town. He further went on to inform them that he was a corrections officer and they were both darn lucky that he hadn't shot them first and asked questions latter! Garage sale or not, these two bozos had just walked into the man's home without even knocking. The man had come to my house to verify that a garage sale was in fact taking place at our address.

We talked for a while and both agreed that garage sales definitely brought out the crazies en masse. It was chilling to think that my attempt to unload our old stuff could have resulted in a double homicide. I suppose it was for that reason that I felt the need to apologize for the two nuts that had invaded the man's privacy. He thanked me for my concern and left.

There was not a cloud in the sky and it was starting to get really hot so I went into the house for a cold drink. I came out to find an elderly man leaning on his cane studying the fifty cent table. He seemed very old and frail with a sallow complexion. His clothes were rumpled and his overall appearance was shabby. He might even have been homeless.

With the question I had been practicing all afternoon I inquired, "See anything you like?"

"Oh, yes. You have a lot of very nice things here," he said through very bad teeth.

I noticed that he was sweating profusely. Concerned, I led him to a chair under a shade tree and sat down next to him. I certainly didn't want him passing out. As we talked he confided that he went to garage sales because if he got a good enough bargain he could sell it for a slightly higher price and so make a little money. I felt really sorry for the old guy. I, for one, planned never to have another garage sale ever again, and this poor man had to use them to put bread on his table.

"Can I get you something to drink?"

"Thank you very much. A cold beer would be great."

That wasn't the drink I had in mind but if that's what the old guy wanted I would accommodate him. It was the least I could do. From all appearances he didn't have two many cold beers left in his future anyway.

Returning to the shade of the tree I marveled at how quickly he drained the can. How do you feel now?"

"Oh, I'm O.K. That beer hit the spot. It's just this darn arthritis that keeps acting up. Well, I should get to my shopping," he said as he struggled to his feet.

As I watched him, the old man moved painfully, bent over, from table to table. He examined everything in minute detail and chose each item as if it were a valuable hidden treasure. It was obvious that he didn't have much money to spend and so had to choose carefully.

After several minutes he had amassed a surprising large amount of items in the center of the driveway. I wondered how he expected to pay for them all, let alone carry his purchases away. Finally, leaning heavily on his cane, he hobbled over to me and announced, "All right young man, I guess that about does it. How much do I owe you?"

A quick appraisal told me that the old guy had accumulated about fifty dollars worth of merchandise. There was no way I could ask him for that much. The man didn't look like he had ever seen fifty dollars in one place. So, in a momentary fit of unexpected compassion I said, "How about ten dollars?"

The old fellow smiled. Then surprisingly, he straightened up as if the price that I announced had been a kind of tonic for his arthritis. He gestured toward the street. Unnoticed by me, a battered old car the exact color of dirt had pulled up and was parked in front of the house. Two scruffy looking young women got out and approached without speaking. One of the women was carrying a flat metal case. When they got to where we were standing the old man signaled to the woman holding the case. As she opened the lid my mouth dropped open at the same time.

The metal case was a cash box and it was crammed full of money. It had separate compartments for bills and change. There must have been hundreds of dollars in there. The old guy, now all business, reached into the box and extracted a ten dollar bill.

"Ten dollars, wasn't it?" he said with a satisfied smile.

I stood there, too surprised to react, as the old man pressed the bill into my hand. He snapped the lid shut on his cash box and gestured to the pile of stuff I had just sold him for practically nothing.

The two women scooped everything up in the blink of an eye and headed back toward their car. The old man marched after them with a new spring in his step. He no longer seemed to be in need of his cane and not a sign of his arthritic problem could be detected as he practically leaped into the front seat of the car. I watched in disbelief as the three sped away.

Unable to make sense out of what had just occurred I went into the house. Seeing my dazed expression my wife asked me what happened. After hearing my explanation she burst out laughing.

"What's so funny?"

"You just ran into a garage sale professional," she chuckled. "He has his own regular ongoing garage sale, probably every weekend, and I'm sure that he also sells on E-Bay. Those folks know exactly what they're doing and they do very well."

I had been taken and I didn't like it one little bit. The sly old man had put on an act to create enough pity so that I would do exactly what I did, practically give away the stuff to him. For some unexplained reason, the thing that I resented the most was the free beer I gave him. No time for second thoughts as my barking dog announced more people coming up the driveway.

After several more grueling hours, finally the garage sale was over. We had sold about three quarters of the stuff and the rest went back into the garage until garbage pickup day. I had just finished counting what I considered the blood money from my sale when my wife inquired, "Where are we going to dinner?"

"Dinner? You're not cooking?" I asked.

"All the preparation for the sale plus the house work I did today really made me tired. Do you mind if we go out?"

So out to dinner to a nice, a.k.a. an expensive restaurant, I went with the wife, my two children and a couple of their friends who the kids implored me to take along. When the bill arrived it totaled just under what the entire profits from my garage sale had come to.

Well, they say, "Easy come. Easy go."

After my sidewalk sales experience I've stuck to my vow to never even consider having another garage sale. I've tried my best to put the entire event behind me. But every once in a while I still think of the old man with the cash box. He should at least have paid me for the beer.

# Moving Daze

### *The Leaning Tower*

I once had an argument with my wife which, I'm convinced, taught me everything that I needed to know about women. Whenever I make this claim in mixed company, every woman in the room bristles.

"Oh, so you know everything that there is to know about us do you?" they scoff.

"Definitely," I say as I explain.

Once while my wife and I were arguing I said to her, "Look, dear, let's settle our disagreement logically."

"Okay," she acquiesced.

"Do you agree with point A?"

"I suppose so," she answered.

"Well then, do you agree with point B?"

She grudgingly responded that she did.

"So," I continued, "if you agree with Point A, and you agree with point B, then point C has to be the inescapable, logical, conclusion."

My bride looked at me with absolute conviction and declared, "I don't care."

That was it. And that's all I believe that any guy needs to know about women. They don't care. Forget logic! They just want what they want when they want it and they are not going to be content until they get it. Most women who hear my explanation agree that this is a lesson every man needs to learn.

When my wife and I began to think about moving to Florida, I took stock of what repairs had to be done to our house before we put it on the market. The first item of concern was our chimney. It was leaning. It wasn't leaning just a little bit; it was leaning more than enough to scare away most potential buyers.

The chimney was at exactly the same angle as when we originally purchased the house and I had been worried about it for years. Way back then my wife and I looked at house after house until we saw the one that she fell in love with.

"But, honey," I said, "the chimney is leaning."

"I don't care," she announced with finality. "I've looked at too many houses already and that's the one I want."

My wife agreed to at least get an engineering report before closing on the property. As we stood in the back yard with our so called expert he looked at the chimney and said, "It's leaning all right and pretty severely, too."

"But why is it leaning?" I asked.

"No way to know."

"Well, is it safe?" I demanded.

Mr. Expert replied, "I can't answer that either. At the angle that it's leaning it could fall tomorrow or stand another hundred years. There is just no way to tell."

I just love it when professional people charge you a fee for stating the obvious. After paying the engineer I had no more information about our questionable pile of bricks than before.

But, having learned my lesson about women in general, and my wife in particular, we went ahead and purchased the house she wanted anyway. The homes on our street were built fairly close together and the chimney was angled toward the neighbor's yard. Fortunately for all, the chimney didn't move an inch during the entire time we owned the house.

Now many years later it was clear to me that our personal Leaning Tower of Pisa had to be dealt with before putting our house on the market.

"We'll have to tear down and rebuild the chimney," I told her.

"Don't be silly," she said. "We'll just take some money off of the sale price and it'll be fine."

"Listen, you can't count on the next woman that falls in love with our house being married to a pushover husband like me."

After a little verbal jousting she finally agreed to call in a bricklayer to give us an estimate.

"How much will you charge me to rebuild the chimney?" I asked the burly man standing in our yard.

He took one look and said, "I don't want the job."

Taken totally off guard, I demanded, "But why not?"

"Look, your chimney is leaning badly and I have no idea why. There could be major foundation issues here. Once I start the demolition there's no telling what problems I could run into. I could be opening a whole can of worms. I'd rather not deal with it."

This was certainly not the reaction I was expecting. The rebuilding of our chimney represented a major payday for this guy and he didn't want the work. If this was the reaction of a professional bricklayer, then I was certain that no prospective buyer would consider our house until our chimney problem was solved.

Since I was having so much trouble convincing my bride of the need for chimney reconstruction, I said to the man, "Would you mind telling my wife what you just told me?"

She was flabbergasted as he explained to her all of his concerns. After the bricklayer left she said, "Well, maybe we do need to fix it after all."

Before we could go ahead with our chimney project we had to deal with the town where we lived. Our community was infamous for making things difficult for the home owner, especially in the area of permitting. No work could begin on our chimney until a permit was issued. No permit would be issued until a professional set of building plans, created by a structural engineer, was submitted and approved by the permitting office of the town. Translation, we had to start spending money.

I picked a structural engineer out of a fancy ad in the phone book. I usually go by the theory that the more impressive the advertisement the greater likelihood of good credentials. Most times I'm right. The engineer came to the house, took pictures of the chimney and two weeks later a set of plans arrived detailing the new construction. Blueprints for the Taj Mahal would pale by comparison with the plans that this man had created for our chimney. The drawings were extremely elaborate, even beautiful. Less beautiful, but just as elaborate was the bill that he included.

The normally fussy permitting officials of our town were impressed enough with the plans to immediately issue us a building permit. I went back to the phonebook to call another bricklayer. The next guy who showed up said he could replace the chimney but the plans were a problem. He told us that to build a chimney according to the impressive drawings would be prohibitively expensive.

Oh this was just great! We had satisfied the town but upset the bricklayers. The next several cement slingers that I called all developed cold feet as well. Either the mystery of the leaning chimney scared them or the elaborate plans, or both. I was getting very concerned. No one seemed to want the job, at least not at a price we could afford. By now fall was coming to an end and winter was fast approaching. I was really feeling the time pressure because I didn't think it would be a great idea to begin a construction project in the snow.

I dialed the structural engineer. "What have you done to me?" I complained. "Most of the guys that I called are afraid of your fancy drawings and those few that aren't are demanding a fortune to do the job."

"You're calling bricklayers, aren't you?" he inquired.

"Of course, who else would I call?"

"You want a mason who builds chimneys, not a bricklayer that just fixes them."

"Like who? I don't know any masons except the ones that belong to the local lodge and I don't think any of those guys even know how to mix cement."

Totally ignoring my sarcasm he continued, "There are just two masons that I would recommend. The best one around is probably all booked up but if he's available I would use him. The second one is also good. I'll give you both numbers".

I called the first one the engineer recommended and was surprised when the man said he was available. He told me to send him a copy of the plans and he would get back to me shortly. I did as he asked but wondered what "The Best" mason on Long Island was going to charge if ordinary bricklayers were demanding a fortune. After two weeks with no response from the mason I called him again.

"I seemed to have misplaced your drawings. They're around here somewhere but I just can't locate them," he unapologetically explained. "Could you send me another set?"

This guy, supposedly "The Best" mason ever, had not only failed to call me back but had lost my drawings besides. This did not exactly inspire confidence that he could do a credible job of rebuilding our chimney. Normally, under these circumstances, I would have told him that his services were not required, but the structural engineer had insisted that this guy was great. So, going purely on that recommendation, I sent off another set of plans to, hopefully, "The Best", but certainly the least organized, mason on Long Island.

A week later he showed up at the house to examine the project firsthand. As we stood together I said, in a thinly veiled attempt to communicate that money was an issue, "Maybe we could just prop the chimney up or put metal straps around it and secure it to the roof.

He smiled a knowing smile and replied, "That chimney weighs at least twenty thousand pounds. Any tie down straps would simply insure that a big part of the roof would be torn off if the chimney did fall, and no props are going to hold up that much weight."

I wondered if this guy was trying to promote an even larger fee out of us with his scare tactics. As he carefully measured our offending structure and wrote copious notes on a clipboard I braced myself for his final estimate. His calculations complete, he turned to me and announced the price we would have to pay for him to take down the entire chimney and build us a new one.

I was shocked. His quote was many thousands of dollars less than what several of the rip-off bricklayers had quoted me. Before he changed his mind I said, "You have a deal," and we shook hands.

I expressed some concern about the weather because winter had begun in earnest and the temperature had fallen. He said that he wasn't too worried and that he and his crew would start the following week.

To insure that the new chimney would seamlessly blend in with the house, the mason told me that he would try to salvage as many of the old bricks as he could and use them in the new construction. This would also save us money on materials. The mason was as good as his reputation and so were his men. The chimney was taken down without incident and with surprising speed.

When the last brick was removed and the very bottom of the chimney was revealed, the mason looked down into the hole and announced, "That was your problem. The footing was inadequate to hold the weight of such a large chimney."

"What's a footing?" I blankly inquired.

"It's a concrete slab that holds the whole thing up. It was much too small and thin to properly support a chimney of this size. Before we start the new construction we'll put one in that will do the job." And then he said something that gave me a chill. "It's lucky that you called me when you did. In my opinion that chimney wasn't going to stand much longer." The thought crossed my mind that it was also very lucky for the neighbor's dog.

A giant slab of reinforced concrete was poured eight feet thick for the new footing. A few days after the cement hardened enough, the mason began to lay the bricks for the new chimney. It was a pleasure to watch him work. He really was an artist with trowel and cement. I was more than satisfied with the way the work was progressing and then… it began to snow. Starting to panic as the temperature continued to drop and the snow increased I asked, "What do 'We' do now?"

I always say 'We' as I question experts when I haven't the slightest idea how to go about solving a problem. It makes me feel like I'm actually part of the solution.

"How can 'We' mix cement when it's below freezing outside?"

"Simple. I'll use boiling water and add a little anti- freeze if necessary." That's what he did and 'We' had the problem solved. I just loved this guy. No obstacle was too great for him to overcome and he had a solution for anything unexpected that came his way.

The mason worked like an iron man in the bitter cold and insisted that his crew do the same. Despite the terrible weather the work was completed exactly on schedule. When they were finished there was no way to tell that the new chimney had not been originally built with the house.

My wife and I were absolutely thrilled with the job the mason and his men had done. Many people only talk a good game but this guy was truly an expert at his craft. If he had run for president I would have voted for him at least twice. This was one time that I was happy to pay the balance of a very large bill. With the chimney rebuilt, our biggest house problem was behind us. I thought.

*Jack of All Trades*

When spring finally arrived it was time to turn my attention to other projects that needed to be completed before putting the house up for sale. We had a long blacktop driveway that was subject to cracking. I had sealed it myself many times but had unfortunately neglected it for the last several years. It was now honeycombed with so many cracks that I decided to get professional help to deal with it.

After the major expense of the chimney I felt that I really needed to get someone at a reasonable price. A small ad in the paper caught my attention. In an attempt to save money I decided to violate my fancy ad, good credentials theory. I read, "Handyman, no job too small."

I thought, "Just the guy I need," and wasted no time in dialing the number. The man who answered the phone said that he was a "Jack of All Trades" and could easily repair the driveway cracks. The amount he said he would charge seemed more than fair for the necessary work. It didn't occur to me at the time that the rest of the "Jack of All Trades" expression is "Master of None".

A man about forty, I'll call him Jack, arrived at the house with his assistant, a young fellow in his twenties. They had with them a five gallon bucket of what Jack said was driveway repair material. Jack told me that he had to go to another job but his assistant was more than competent to complete the job in a single afternoon. He set the young man to work, said that he would be back later to collect his pay, and off he went. I watched as the assistant carefully filled several of the cracks with the material from the bucket and smoothed them with a trowel. He was a diligent worker and seemed to be doing a good job and so I returned to the house and left him to his task.

Several hours later the job was completed. The kid was tired but proud of the work he had done. Every crack in the driveway was filled with shiny black filler. Jack showed up on schedule to retrieve his assistant and get paid. I asked him when he thought the crack filler would be dry enough for us to drive on. He said that we should be able to use our driveway after twenty four hours. I tipped the young man who had worked so hard, and paid Jack the agreed on price. He thanked me and they left.

A full day later I went out to the driveway. I wanted to be sure that the crack filler had completely dried before we moved our cars so I knelt down and touched a finger to one of the cracks. As I lifted my hand a string of the black material came up with it just like a long strand of black chewing gum. I touched another one with the same result. It was more than twenty four hours and the stuff had not dried at all.

The young man had left the mostly empty can of driveway filler in my shed. I wanted to read the instructions on the label to see how long it would take to finally dry. Jack was obviously wrong about the twenty-four hours. On the way to the shed I had to hop scotch around multiple cracks so as not to get the sticky black stuff on my shoes. Once inside the shed I tried to read the label on the can. It wasn't easy as the contents had dripped all over and obscured most of the label. As I strained to read it, suddenly, to my horror, I was able to make out the partially covered words, "ROOFING PITCH"!

This stuff wasn't driveway crack filler at all. I knew about Roofing Pitch. It was only used on roofs as waterproofing. It never dries. It's not supposed to. It's essentially non-drying tar. With mounting rage I looked over my driveway at the countless cracks filled to the brim with roofing pitch. To think that I had actually tipped the kid for doing such a good job made me even madder.

I couldn't even storm into the house because I had to carefully avoid all the wet tar on the way to the phone. Totally enraged, I called Mr. Jack of All Trades and demanded to know why he had essentially ruined my driveway.

Unperturbed, he casually said, "To tell you the truth, I'm not that experienced with driveways. The man at the big box store told me to use the stuff I brought and so that's what I did. Sorry if it didn't work out." And he hung up.

I decided right then that the world is full of idiots: the man in the big box store for recommending roofing pitch to fill driveway cracks, Mr. Jack of All Trades for using it, and me for hiring Jack in the first place. You truly do get what you pay for.

But there was no time for regrets. The countless tar filled cracks were glistening in the morning sunlight and I had a really big problem with no idea how to solve it.

My first thought was to cover the cracks with sand. I figured the sand would stick to the tar and create a dry enough surface to drive on. I took a handful of sand, poured it on the first crack and pressed down. As I lifted my hand the sand and tar came up with it in a gooey, sandy, mess. This was clearly not the solution. I now was sure that I couldn't put anything on top of the tar because the stuff was never, ever going to dry. I was fast coming to the realization that I had been dreading. The only way to fix what Mr. Jack of All Trades had done to my driveway was to remove all of the roofing pitch. But how to do that was the big question.

I thought, "Maybe I can use some kind of solvent." But there were hundreds of tar filled cracks to deal with, and Jack's assistant had used almost five gallons of the stuff. To dissolve that much roofing pitch would require many more gallons of solvent. I didn't think my neighbors would appreciate a toxic black river running down their street very much.

There was nothing for it but to scrape the stuff out of each and every crack by hand. I got a thin pointed masonry trowel, a pile of old newspapers and a large garbage can from the shed. I knelt down and attacked the first of the cracks. I scraped out as much of the black goo as I could. The pitch stuck like glue to anything it touched. I wiped the trowel off on a scrap of newspaper and scraped some more. This truly was a nightmarish job.

After a few minutes of scraping I was satisfied that crack number one was essentially as tar free as it was going to get. I stood up and surveyed the rest of the driveway. There seemed to be an endless number of tar filled cracks to deal with. But it wouldn't have mattered if there were a million of them. I knew that, until all the roofing pitch was removed, my driveway was useless. The only good news was I hadn't hired Jack to build us a chimney. Resigned to my fate, I approached crack number two and applied my scraping and wiping technique. Then, crack after crack, scraping and wiping, wiping and scraping, I attacked the rest of the driveway like a madman. After one full week of back breaking, crack scraping labor, I was able to pronounce the driveway free of the never drying goo. It's lucky for him that I didn't have magical powers because, as I worked, I wished all sorts of terrible things on Mr. Jack of All Trades. Some of those things involved more novel and exotic uses for roofing pitch.

This time I went myself to the big box store and bought several calking tubes of driveway crack filler. I was sure that's what they were because the labels said so. I suppose that Jack had either been too lazy to read the label on the can of Pitch or was just plain illiterate. I filled every single crack and in less than twenty four hours the crack filler was dry. After applying a coat of driveway sealer the job was done and so was I. Upon reflection, the dismal fact was that it took Jack's assistant just one afternoon to mess up my driveway but almost two weeks for me to fix it.

The chimney had been a major home run, but with the driveway I had totally struck out. So, if I considered things in baseball terms, I was still batting five hundred. While this made me feel a little better psychologically it did nothing for my aching back. Anyway, I had done a terrific job. The driveway never looked so good.

Having developed a handyman phobia as a result of my experience with Mr. Jack of All Trades, I decided to tackle as many of the remaining house repairs as I could myself. Several months later I pronounced our home ready for the market.

## Black Rain

By now we had a place in Florida and were anxious to move. The realtor that we hired was a dynamic woman with many years of real estate experience. After surveying the house and grounds she said, "You need a new roof. The one you've got should be replaced."

My wife and I were united in our response. "No way," we told the realtor, "we've spent enough money already. Anyone interested in buying our house can negotiate the price to cover the cost of a new roof."

"All right," she responded, "but I think you're making a mistake."

The problem was that, through the years, two roofs had been put on over the original one. Three layers of shingles were the maximum allowed by code. Before a new roof could be installed all three layers of the old roofing shingles had to first be removed. We just didn't want to deal with the expense and mess of dealing with yet another large project. In all other respects our house was beautiful. It was a Tudor style with lots of charm. Expecting a quick sale, we put the house on the market and waited for a buyer to fall in love with the place. Six months later we were still waiting with no takers anywhere near our price. It was the beginning of the real estate market "crash" and very few properties in our small town were selling.

We decided we would just move to our Florida home anyway. We could fly back for the closing when the house was sold. The realtor kept insisting that the reason we hadn't had a buyer yet was because of the old roof. Finally she convinced us to replace it.

The man from the roofing company told us he had a large crew and it would only take them one day to remove the old shingles. He said that, barring unforeseen weather problems, the new roof could probably be put on the next day. He guaranteed that the entire job would take three days at the most to complete. We signed a contract for the work to begin immediately.

The roofing crew arrived and there were a lot of them as promised. They swarmed over the roof like so many mountain goats, and by the end of the day three layers of roofing shingles were deposited in a large dumpster. Two days later our house had a gorgeous new roof. We tipped the men and paid the balance of the bill. Since the roof was the last item on our repair list we felt free to hire a moving company and set the date for the move.

I was in the kitchen when my wife decided to go upstairs and start the packing. She opened the door to one of two large walk-in attics. All of a sudden I heard her yell and I rushed upstairs. She was sobbing as I approached. My attention was on her so I didn't immediately notice why she was crying.

When she calmed down enough to speak she said, "Look at what the roofers have done."

What I saw when I looked across the attic, deposited over all of our accumulated possessions, was a thick layer of black granules. It was the consistency of sugar and it was everywhere.

At first I couldn't figure out what the stuff was and then it hit me. It was asphalt particles from the old roofing shingles. But how had what I dubbed this "Black Rain" gotten into our attic? Since the attic was unfinished, the source of the granules was revealed as I studied the ceiling.

Our Tudor House was built in 1926 when they used tongue and groove boards instead of plywood as the support for the shingles. Over the years these boards had shrunk and spaces had developed between each one. When the roofing crew shoveled the three layers of shingles off the roof much of the dried asphalt particles sifted down through those spaces and onto everything in the attic.

A check of the second attic revealed the same depressing situation. The shed and garage, which were also full of things that needed to be packed, had suffered the same fate.

Once again I found myself picking up the phone in a rage as I dialed the roofing contractor. When I told him the situation he said, "Oh, yes, the roofs of a lot of those old houses were built with boards instead of plywood. I should have remembered that. So sorry." His lame apology was a small consolation considering the position that he had put us in.

The moving company was due to arrive in a week and a last minute schedule change was not possible. Under normal circumstances seven days would have been more than enough time to pack our stuff. But this was not a normal situation. The Black Rain had been deposited on everything.

Instead of merely putting things into boxes as we had expected to do, we had to first vacuum the stuff off and, in the case of clothing, both vacuum and wash the item before packing it. And all this had to be done before the movers arrived. I was too upset to even play my baseball batting average game to cheer myself up. Anyway, what was the point? I sure wasn't batting five hundred anymore. The roofing contractor was yet another person who benefitted from my lack of magical powers as I heaped curses on his head while wielding my shop vac in the attics and garage. I might have been able to get him to send a cleaning crew if I hadn't already paid him in full. A lesson learned too late. But who could have expected Black Rain inside the house?

Most people agree that moving is generally an unpleasant experience. They say that the stress level can even be compared to a death in the family. As I worked my shop vac my bride worked the washer, dryer and somehow, acting together, we were done when the movers arrived. But I have to say, getting ready for our move almost killed us. The only saving grace was that it was winter. Had the Black Rain descended on us in the summer, the asphalt granules would have melted in the attic heat and everything would have been ruined.

## *Location, Location, Location*

When all of our stuff was safely packed and headed for Florida, we decided to visit a friend of ours. He was also planning to move and we wanted to say goodbye. His house was in a residential neighborhood in Brooklyn that was located, as they say in real estate, in a hot area. This friend had lived overseas for most of his working life and had rented his home out during that time. As we pulled up in front of his house I took note of how sad and dilapidated the building looked. The paint was peeling and the shingles of the old roof were curled with age. The overgrown lawn consisted entirely of weeds that were a couple of feet high. Emerging from the weeds was a wobbly stick on which was tacked a homemade "For Sale" sign with a phone number. The sign looked as if a child had written it in crayon. We stood at the door and I noticed several rusty screws lying on the ground near a dirty welcome mat. As we rang the bell I wondered how my friend ever expected to sell this place in its present condition.

The house didn't look much better on the inside. After a pleasant lunch I suggested as tactfully as I could that he might want to make some improvements to help sell the place.

"It's not necessary," he said. "Right now this area is red hot. I've only had the sign up a couple of days."

"You're not working with a realtor?"

"No, I don't want to pay the commission."

"Well okay, but you should at least pick up those rusty screws near the welcome mat," I gently observed.

After lunch we said goodbye and wished each other well. As we drove away I said to my wife, "I bet he's going to be sitting with that place forever."

"Well, maybe he'll get lucky."

"No chance," I countered, "not with that wreck of a house. Besides, he's not even using a realtor."

Two weeks later my friend called with unbelievable news. His home had sold for his full asking price. And there was something else. A few days after he agreed to sell, a woman called him and said that she wanted to buy the house. When he told her that he had already agreed to sell it to someone else she said, "I'll give you fifty thousand dollars more than they offered you."

My friend observed, "You haven't even been in the house yet to look around."

"It doesn't matter. I want to be on the block you're on."

My friend told her that he felt he had to honor the agreement he made.

I asked him, "How could you so easily turn down an extra fifty thousand dollars?"

He told me that, besides being a matter of personal ethics, he was content with the price he had gotten. He felt he had sold the house for a small fortune that was many times more than he had paid for it thirty years before.

Another three months went by before our beautiful Tudor home also was finally purchased. After paying the real estate commission and deducting the cost of all the repairs we had made, I figured that we ended up with about half of what my friend had gotten for his house. We had spent two years getting our place ready at great physical, financial and emotional cost and our friend had not done a single thing to prepare his home for sale. In real estate, when you're hot, you're hot; and it's always going to be about "location, location, location". But he was a good friend and I was happy for us both. Still, knowing him, I bet he never even got around to picking up those screws.

# Dream House

Some years ago I bought a popular magazine that showcased the best places in America where one might want to retire. One of the publication's picks jumped out at me. They described an area in Florida that they claimed was "the most affordable waterfront community in the country."

"Imagine," the article went on, "you can have your boat on a lift right in your own back yard at a very reasonable cost."

Wow! This was something that I had always dreamed of but was impossible for us to even consider as long as we lived on Long Island. So I mentally filed away this information until the day when our retirement was imminent.

I shared my thinking with my very best friend, a lifelong New Yorker. "Florida, isn't that where old people go to die?" he unkindly observed.

"You don't understand," I responded. "It's not the Early Bird Special part of Florida. We are going to the west coast, on the gulf side where there's a much more active life style. You know, boating, fishing and all."

"And what about the hurricanes?" my buddy cheerfully inquired.

"Oh, I've thoroughly researched that situation. The part of Florida where we're going has not had a hurricane in over forty-three years," I informed him. He wasn't convinced but, not wanting to rain on my parade, my good friend decided to put his anti-Florida bias on hold.

Finally, the day of our retirement arrived. My wife and I told each other that since we had both worked hard our entire lives that we deserved a dream house and opted to have a home built in the area of Florida with the promised affordable waterfront. Several years had passed since the magazine article was written and, not surprisingly, the place turned out to be less affordable than it had been. But there were many canals leading to a gorgeous harbor that was teeming with all kinds of fish. The local real estate offices marketed the community with headlines proclaiming, "Welcome to Paradise." For us, coming from the frozen north, it really did seem like it. So we decided that this was the place to be.

We had heard horror stories about how some Florida builders swindle their clients and therefore we carefully interviewed several before deciding on one. We ultimately chose a builder that came highly recommended. He emphasized two major points at our first meeting. "Don't change my subcontractors because they've been with me for years and I know that they do good work. And, watch out for the upgrades; they'll kill you."

In the beginning we ignored his advice about the upgrades until the bills started to arrive in bunches. Then we realized that maybe we didn't deserve quite everything we thought we had wanted and scaled things down a bit.

The subcontractors were another matter. Yes, it was true that most of them had been with him for years but he neglected to mention that a few others had just recently been employed for the building of our house. This costly fact we only found out after construction was complete. The most glaring example of this was the landscape contractor. She turned out to be as slick and untrustworthy as any of the snakes that would later slither through the overpriced and sad looking garden that she ended up creating for us.

I had seen many landscapers on T.V. take their clients to nurseries to pick out the plants of their choosing. When I asked our landscaper if she would be doing the same with us, she said that wasn't the way she worked. This, the first of several red flags, we totally missed. The builder had informed us that she was great and we took him at his word. Big mistake!

Since we were in Florida, my wife wanted palm trees. The landscaper, who I later dubbed, "Snake Lady," said that we couldn't have any.

"And why not?" my wife demanded to know.

Snake lady informed us that because most palm trees were not native to Florida they had no points assigned to them and would not meet our point quota.

"What in the world are you talking about?" I asked.

Snake Lady explained that, depending upon the size of the building lot, the county where we were located assigned a certain number of points that must be used before a Certificate of Occupancy would be issued. We could accomplish this by planting approved types and sizes of native trees to use up the points. The problem was we felt that most of the native trees were really ugly. It seemed that virtually none of the plants that we wanted met the county's point requirements.

Our building lot was assigned thirteen of these troublesome points. Each point was valued at a hundred dollars each. Snake Lady said that if I wanted to I could write a check to the county for the total dollar amount of the points and I would then be free to plant whatever I wished. This sounded to me suspiciously like a kind of landscape racket the county was running. Snake Lady knew very well that I was not about to spend thirteen hundred dollars and get nothing in return.

She also warned us against buying plants on our own. "You don't want a big box store kind of landscaping do you?" she asked. As it later turned out that's precisely what we should have done. The larger garden centers offer a one year guarantee on all of their plants. Snake Lady guaranteed nothing. Her warning was just a ploy so that she could overcharge us for her substandard shrubbery. But trusting the recommendation of our builder, we didn't know any of this at the time.

The problem was that neither my wife nor I knew anything much about plants. All we were sure of was that we wanted attractive landscaping to complement our dream house. To that end we had upgraded the landscape allotment to a virtually obscene level. So it was really puzzling when the Snake Lady kept telling us that there was not enough money in the budget to accommodate most of the special features we had wanted. However, she did make elaborate sketches of her vision for our property. We were so impressed with the artwork that we signed off on the drawings. But where the drawings were beautiful, unfortunately, the finished landscaping was not. In fact, it was awful. The shrubs looked sickly and the trees appeared to be near death.

All complaints were met with horticultural excuses. "Oh don't worry," she said, "plants get stressed when they are transplanted. They'll perk up soon enough."

I don't know about other people but when anyone tells me not to worry, that's when my worry mode goes into overdrive.

Our builder supported Snake Lady's view that the sad looking plants would soon recover. Not convinced, but with few options at this point, we decided to take a wait and see attitude.

Our house was completed about a month later and we flew down for the final inspection. As we were having our walk-through with the builder, Hurricane Charley was rapidly approaching the coast of Florida.

The house was just about everything we wanted and even had hurricane proof impact glass on all but two of the windows. When we entered the garage I spotted several large aluminum panels leaning against the wall. I turned to the builder and asked, "What are those things?"

"Oh, those are your hurricane shutters for the two windows that aren't impact glass."

"Well, isn't there a storm coming? Shouldn't you put them up?"

"Not necessary. The weatherman just tries to scare everybody. We don't get hurricanes down here. In fact we haven't had one in over forty years."

"Well, I'm the nervous type. Please put them up anyway."

Unconcerned, as we continued touring the house he said without much conviction, "I'll see what I can do."

Outside, the landscaping did not look any better than it had a month earlier. In fact, it looked a whole lot worse. The builder again told us to be patient and that the plants should recover.

After the walk-through we drove over to Florida's east coast to spend some time with my mother. We began to get more anxious watching the local news as it was announced that the hurricane would hit within the next few days. The weatherman could not pinpoint the exact spot where the storm would make landfall. But since our area had seemed to be immune from hurricanes for decades we were not too worried. Our concern increased slightly as the reports stated that the storm would probably land about a few hundred miles to the north of where our house was located. Close, but still far enough away for comfort.

"It's a lucky thing that I'm such a good researcher," I bragged to my wife. "Thank goodness we don't have to worry. I'd hate to be those people living anywhere else on the gulf side of Florida."

We awoke to terrible news. The weather report now said that the storm had taken a sudden unexpected turn and was now headed for our area. Since our house was in a development managed by a building association I called there and asked the woman who answered the phone if there was any chance of our getting water in our brand new home.

"Absolutely," she said. "The houses here are at thirteen feet above sea level. If this category four storm does hit, the tidal surge is predicted to be about twenty feet."

"Tidal surge? What's a Tidal Surge?" I asked.

"It's like a tidal wave created by hurricane force winds that can push the water up the canals for miles. Since you are at a thirteen foot elevation a twenty foot high tidal surge would dump seven feet of water in your house."

I hung up in total shock. I had never heard of a tidal surge before. Why hadn't the magazine article on where to retire said anything about them? "Oh yes," I remembered, "we aren't supposed to get hurricanes so there had been no need to mention the possibility of surges."

As the day went on the news got progressively worse. When the weatherman began referring to our area potentially as "Ground Zero", I started to feel some surges of my own. At this point I was psychologically in really bad shape. I had never felt this low before. My wife suggested that we go out to dinner and take a break from the news for a little while. I remember that when the food arrived it had no taste. When the waitress asked what we would like for desert I told her to see if there was a cup of hemlock in the kitchen.

That night I went to bed feeling like a condemned man with only one day left. I couldn't get our builder on the phone and had no idea if he had bothered to put up the hurricane shutters on our two windows not made of impact glass. I remembered that he hadn't seemed very concerned about them at the time. I was tormented by the idea that if he had neglected to put up those shutters the unprotected windows would be blown out. I had been told by someone that once hurricane force winds get into a house the pressure inside would cause the roof to lift right off.

All attempts by the family to console me fell on deaf ears. When it was suggested that we could get lucky and the storm just might pass us by I all but shouted, "And what does 'Ground Zero' mean to you?"

My concerns about the landscaping now seemed totally irrelevant. I couldn't help thinking that my bride and I had put a good portion of our life savings into building a dream house that just might end up under seven feet of water. The next morning Hurricane Charley made a direct hit on our area with incredible force. The weather report labeled the storm a category four hurricane but with wind gusts exceeding two hundred miles per hour; the local people knew that it was actually a category five, the strongest kind of hurricane there is.

The final straw for me came when the weather channel kept showing the street sign that used to be in front of our development. It had been knocked down and was lying in a water filled ditch. To insure that my blood pressure remained at an all time high, the rotten weatherman kept referring to our area, over and over again, as "Ground Zero". I was sure that my dream of living the good life in Florida had been shattered forever.

To make matters even worse, if the storm had hit just a few days earlier the damage would have been the builder's problem. Since we'd already completed our walk-through the builder had been paid in full. Any loss was now totally ours to bear, and our homeowners' insurance had a huge hurricane deductible.

"What terrible luck I have," I thought. "My New York friend was right. I should never have come to Florida." I was really feeling sorry for myself.

On one of our trips while the house was under construction I had become acquainted with our new next door neighbors. They were wonderful people who unwisely had decided to ride out the storm. Fearing the worst, I called them to find out if they were all right and also to see if our house was still standing. From all the news reports, our community, the place that wasn't supposed to get hurricanes, had gotten totally blasted.

So I was greatly relieved to hear that my neighbors were fine and our dream house had only sustained relatively minor damage. My wife and I drove back to Florida's west coast to see for ourselves.

Had my neighbor not told me that our house was essentially okay, the drive through the community would have convinced me that our home was a total loss. Everywhere we looked all we saw were scenes of total devastation. There was no electricity as all the power lines were down. Roofs were ripped off and large trees had crashed down onto many houses. Big palms had simply been sheared off like matchsticks. Driving was extremely hazardous as no traffic lights were working and the roads were littered with debris of every kind.

When we finally got to our development we passed the street sign that the T.V. weatherman had spotlighted in his "Ground Zero" reports. The sign was still there in the ditch. The iron gate at the entrance to our development had been torn off its hinges and was just lying on the grass. The force of the wind must have been incredible.

As we approached our house we were relieved to see that we had gotten off easy, probably because our home was built to the newest and strongest building codes. There were several missing roof tiles but, since they were mainly there for beauty and to protect the actual waterproofing under them, this wasn't a real problem. All the windows had held and our builder had thankfully gotten around to putting up the hurricane shutters on the two windows that needed them. He had built us a beautiful solid house after all.

The greatest damage was to the screened pool enclosure that in Florida they call a pool cage. The force of the wind had literally torn it out of the cement and flung the twisted supports and screening into the pool. A scrap metal dealer later removed it without charging us for his service and our insurance company covered the damages. All in all we were O.K.

Most of the rest of the community was not so fortunate. Blue tarps covering damaged roofs could be seen everywhere you looked. Most pool cages were mangled and down. Windows everywhere were blown out.

Luckily for us the tidal surge never happened. A hurricane spins, sort of like a giant tornado. This storm had been spinning in exactly the right direction to push water out of the harbor instead of up the canals. Had the storm been rotating in the opposite direction the tidal surge would have occurred for sure and our home would have been lost. Our fortunes had rested on a kind of hurricane roulette wheel. Thankfully we had won.

The landscaping now looked like, well, like a hurricane had hit it. It had never been good to begin with but now it was really terrible. The fellow who cut our grass could not believe how much we had been charged. He knew plants and he said that Snake Lady had not given us even a small fraction of what she should have and what we had paid for. We didn't drag Snake Lady into court although we briefly considered it. What better defense could she have for her shoddy work than to simply say the cheap sickly plants she put in didn't survive because of the ferocious storm?

We moved into our house a few weeks later when power was restored to the community. I immediately set to work to renovate our landscaping. While shopping at a local nursery for replacement shrubs I recounted my experience with Snake Lady to the owner. He laughed and said, "She used to work for me. That woman is famous around here for cheating people."

Enraged, I rushed home to call our builder. I snarled, "You know, your wonderful landscaper – well, I just found out that she's famous for cheating people. It's common knowledge. What did you do to us?"

"I didn't know that. I've only used her a few times and she was good. I won't use her again."

When I reminded him about his claim that all of his subs were supposedly with him for years and were totally dependable, his silence spoke volumes. I would get no satisfaction from him in the landscape department. My wife told me to stop obsessing about Snake Lady and the builder and get on with the renovation. In return for this sage advice I rewarded her with the palms that she wanted.

Ultimately things began to get back to normal as the community got on with the slow work of rebuilding. Eventually I replaced all of the landscaping myself. The plants came from the big box stores and every one came with a guarantee. The results were beautiful.

My bride thinks that part of her wifely duties is to set me straight from time to time. Her technique is direct and usually not very subtle. Our house, built to the newest building code, sustained very little damage compared to many of our neighbors. Nevertheless, one day I was lamenting my lousy luck. I complained to my wife, "I can't believe it, no hurricanes in over forty years and as soon as I build a house here this had to happen."

"And why do you always think it's all about you?" queried my bride. "The entire community was practically wrecked and our house came through basically all right. Why don't you stop complaining and start counting your blessings?"

I thought about it a moment, gave her a big kiss, and did just that.

# Angel

Those summers that we spent in the country when I was a kid I will always remember as a gift my mother had given me, for which I'll always be grateful. The Catskills were a great place to learn to fish, enjoy the outdoors and commune with nature. Years later though, I gravitated more toward salt water angling. Fishing on lakes and rivers was very relaxing, but it was salt water that provided the excitement that I was after as an adult.

The home that we were building in Florida was still in its planning stages when my wife and I flew down to meet with the builder and several of his subcontractors. Since school was out for the summer our teenage son went with us. After the meeting we were driving back to the hotel when we passed a local tackle shop.

On a whim, we decided to go in and get some information about the local fishing. We had no plans to fish but were just interested in learning about the area. The tackle shop was not one of those glitzy ones that you see today but was rather a throwback to a time when fisherman hung out in such salty places swapping fishing stories and trading lies. Occasionally they might even buy something as well. My son immediately struck up a conversation with a friendly young man behind the counter. It turned out that he was not an employee of the store but was a regular customer who volunteered to help out part time in the shop.

He seemed very knowledgeable about the fishing in our area and was happy to share what he knew with us. My wife was getting anxious to leave and we started moving toward the door when the young man abruptly called after us, "Hey, you guys want to go snook fishing with me?"

My wife immediately decided for us. I hate it when she does that. She made direct eye contact with me and began an almost imperceptible negative head shake that I had become familiar with over the years. This specialized signaling technique of hers is designed to avoid a public argument and can be detected only by experienced married men.

Ignoring her, my son and I walked back to the counter and I asked the guy, "What's a snook?"

My bride of many years now gave me one of the more dangerous looks in her arsenal meant to silently communicate, "Don't you dare even think about it, Buster."

The young man was fortunately totally unaware of this unspoken marital communication as he held forth on the joys of snook fishing.

"Snook," he told us, "are among the most prized and sought after food and sport fish in our area. They are great fighters and can reach a weight of up to sixty pounds, although five to twenty pounders are more common."

The pleasant young man said that his name was Angel and that he had moved down to Florida from the Bronx, New York, about four years earlier. In that time he said that he had become an expert snook fisherman. He told us that while many people had never caught even a single snook, he had personally landed over two thousand of these elusive fish. As our conversation progressed my wife continued to look daggers at me.

Angel informed us that the tide would be just right at eleven o'clock that night. If we wanted to catch some snook we should meet him at the tackle shop at that time and he'd guide us to his favorite fishing spot. When I told him that my son and I hadn't brought any fishing rods, he said that it wasn't a concern since he had enough equipment for each of us. As we walked out to the parking lot together we passed Angel's SUV. Inside his car, suspended by two canvas slings, were several fishing rods hanging down right across where passengers would normally sit. Angel's car was a total fishmobile. Fishing clearly was not just his passion, fishing was his life.

When Angel and I exchanged cell phone numbers I thought my wife's head was going to explode right there in the parking lot. I told him that I couldn't promise but we would try and meet him that night. Angel replied that if we didn't show up he would just fish by himself, but he really preferred the company.

As we got back into our car my bride, no longer able to contain her upset, turned to me in a fury and hissed through clenched teeth, "Are you crazy? Correct me if I'm wrong. Did I just hear you agree to go fishing at eleven o'clock tonight, at a place you've never been, with a stranger named Angel that you just met a few minutes ago?"

"Yup, that's right, you did,"

"What is the matter with you? You don't know this man. Suppose he wants to rob you, or worse?"

Angel waved to us as we were driving away and I took this opportunity to take a second look at him. He was a solidly built young guy with a swarthy complexion and he sported one gold tooth. He had been pleasant enough to talk with but I had to admit that gold tooth did make him look just a little like a bandit. It never occurred to me that Angel might have an ulterior motive for his invitation. He seemed genuine enough and that car of his was the fishingest vehicle that I had ever seen. Nevertheless, my wife had a point. Even though I thought Angel was okay, I had to agree that there was some element of risk in going night fishing with a perfect stranger.

I turned to my son and asked, "Well, what do you think? Should we go?"

Without hesitation my son, a big strong teenager, responded, "Sure, Dad. First off, I've got your back. And second, the guy's talking snook here!"

My bride promptly pronounced us both crazy and asked, "And what about the kitchen subcontractor that we're supposed to meet with at eight thirty tomorrow morning? We came down here to build a house, remember? After all, there are priorities."

"I know," I insisted, "and that's why my son and I are going snook fishing with an expert. Don't worry about the kitchen guy. I'll be sure to be back at the hotel in time for the meeting and I can always take a nap later in the day to make up for any lost sleep."

Seeing that fishing frenzy had totally possessed her men my wife finally gave up but made one final demand.

"If you really are nuts enough to do this then go ahead but on one condition. I want you to take your cell phone with you and give me a call every hour."

I immediately agreed and the matter for the moment was settled. My wife wasn't thrilled but a limited peace once again returned to Happy Valley.

At exactly eleven that night my son and I pulled into the deserted parking lot of the fishing tackle store. True to his word, Angel was there waiting next to his fishmobile. He told us to follow him and that it would take about twenty minutes to get to where the snook were no doubt hungrily waiting. And so off we went. Now that I was actually following Angel down an unfamiliar road the concerns that my wife had voiced earlier once again popped into my head. She was worried that we were meeting with a potential mugger. Was I stupidly risking the safety of myself and my son just to catch a couple of fish? I had to agree that Angel did look a little like a bandit. The thought briefly crossed my mind to forget the snook, turn the car around, and head back to the hotel.

I quickly shook off this line of negative thinking by deciding to not let my wife's female hysteria become my own. I prided myself on being a good judge of character and Angel seemed all right to me.

We drove for another ten minutes until the road began to border the harbor. Suddenly, on an overpass above the water, Angel signaled us to pull off onto the shoulder. We parked illegally, right behind him.

Angel got out and smiled, flashing that gold tooth again.

"Well, this is the spot."

"Can we just park on the shoulder like this?" I asked.

"Don't worry about it. Everybody fishes on this side of the bridge. I know most of the cops. The police won't bother us if we park here. The other side of the road is where they give out the tickets. I learned that the hard way."

I wondered how Angel had become acquainted with so many policemen. Were these more fishing buddies, or could they have been his probation officers? There was no way to know.

"There you go again," I thought, "letting your wife's hysteria start to get the better of you."

My fears were abruptly dispelled as Angel handed both my son and me sturdy fishing rods. He told us that we would have to climb down about twenty feet over some large boulders to the sea wall below.

The light was dim under the bridge as we carefully made our descent over the rocks. Just on the off chance that my wife's fears about Angel were justified, I kept looking around for a possible ambush by bandits.

We managed to make it safely to the bottom and began to fish from the sea wall. We cast the jointed swimming lures Angel had provided for us with no resulting strikes.

One of my problems is that I'm a very suggestible person. Angel had seemed so sure about when the fish would start biting that, once again, the nagging thought occurred to me that this fishing trip might have been just a ruse to get us to this deserted spot so that we could be robbed. I strained my eyes in the gloom and scanned the surrounding rocks for any potential bad guys. None could be seen. Again I forced myself to dismiss for the moment any concerns about Angel as nothing more than the result of my wife's powers of suggestion.

I asked, "Angel, where are the fish that you promised us?"

He glanced at his watch and said, "The tide's not right just yet. Give it a little more time."

Several minutes later Angel announced that he had a hit. He cast again and said that another fish had attacked his lure.

"Angel, I keep hearing about hits but I don't see any fish yet."

As I spoke to him I kept a sharp eye on the rocks above us for possible trouble. My wife, it seemed, had planted the seed of doubt about Angel much deeper than I had first realized.

Just at that moment all my concerns were eliminated. Angel's rod bent double as a huge snook took his lure. After a terrific fight that lasted several minutes Angel hoisted a fish more than two feet long over the sea wall. He carefully unhooked it and returned it to the water, explaining that the snook season was closed. We wouldn't be keeping any fish. This night was to be strictly for fun and would be an exclusively catch and release event.

On the very next cast Angel was into another snook even bigger than the first one. But my son and I, with the same rods and lures, were being completely snookered by the snook.

I turned to Angel and asked, "What are we doing wrong?"

He studied our technique for a moment and expertly proclaimed, "You're both reeling too fast. Slow down your retrieve."

As soon as we did as instructed we were both instantly into fish. Angel really knew his stuff.

Now that we had the technique down and the tide was moving fast the fishing moved even faster. I have never seen anything like the snook fishing we had that night on the seawall. One of us had a fish on at any given moment. All of the fish were huge and each put up a terrific fight. I hooked one snook that was so big that leaning back on the rod as hard as I could, I couldn't budge him. After a short but violent struggle he shook the lure which whistled right past my ear. Oh, it was a glorious night and one I will never forget!

In the middle of fighting a fish my cell phone rang.

"Oh my gosh," I thought. In all the excitement I had completely forgotten the time and my promise to call my wife. She wasn't quite hysterical but close to it.

"Why didn't you call me?" she demanded, her voice shaking. "I thought that you both might be killed. You promised to call me every hour and…. "

"Sorry, dear," I said, cutting her off. "I'll explain later". "I can't talk to you now". "We're catching snook!"

And I hung up.

Normally, hanging up on my wife like that, in the state she was in, would have been a more dangerous move than if I had really encountered bandits. But this night I was not about to give up even a minute of the best fishing I had ever experienced.

The action continued fast and furious. I lost track of all the fish we caught and released. Only when the tide began to change, in the early hours of the morning, did the fishing slow down. It was during this slack time that Angel shared a dream with us. He said that, while he was an expert shore fisherman, he really wanted to buy a boat and make his living as a professional fishing guide. He told us that he had almost saved up enough money to make his dream a reality.

The tide by now had fully changed and the fish abruptly stopped biting. The sun was just coming up and it was way past time to get back to the hotel. We thanked Angel profusely for the fishing experience of a lifetime as my son and I reluctantly headed back to face the wifely and motherly music.

Kids get all the breaks. My wife and I did meet with the kitchen subcontractor that morning while our son slept soundly back at the hotel. I don't remember much of what was said at that meeting as I was still reeling in endless snook in my mind. My wife must have paid better attention because we ended up with a pretty nice kitchen.

As for Angel, not long after our house was completed he got his captain's license and his boat. Ultimately he rose to the pinnacle of his profession, becoming one of the most beloved and respected fishing guides in the community. Periodically we waved to him when he passed our dock as he expertly guided his clients to fishing experiences they would never forget.

Besides the fishing, one of the things that I enjoyed most was being right about Angel. He turned out to be a really terrific guy. My wife, who truly believes that her intuition is almost infallible, was forced to admit that this time it had completely failed her and she was relieved that it had.

He may have looked sort of like a bandit and his invitation to guide two perfect strangers after dark may have seemed more than a little fishy, but that night on the sea wall catching snook after snook, Capt. Angel sure lived up to his name.

# Family Ties

## *Chain of Command*

On a warm summer day, on the Eastern Shore of Maryland, most of my wife's relatives were gathered at the site of a tragic fire that cost the lives of one of her cousins and an uncle. The fire had been caused by a short in some wiring and the frame house had burned to the ground. On this particular afternoon the family had assembled to sift through the ashes in an attempt to find any possible mementoes. They were also there to clear some tree stumps since a new house was to be built on this site.

On an oversized farm tractor sat my wife's great uncle, the acknowledged patriarch of the family. He was trying to pull a big stump out of the ground using a heavy chain attached to a steel crossbar on the back of his tractor. About twenty five family members had formed a circle to watch as this venerable old gentleman made his contribution to the new construction. Unfortunately the stump was stubbornly resisting the best efforts of the diesel powered machine. The strain must have been great because the chain suddenly pulled off of the tractor's crossbar.

My wife of one year leaned over and whispered to me, "Go tie the chain back on."

I shook my head strongly in the negative. I was feeling self-conscious as I had barely just met her relatives. Sure I had seen many of them at our wedding but I didn't even remember most of their names, and they didn't really know me yet.

Here I was a guy from Brooklyn in the middle of Maryland farm country. Surrounded by her entire family I certainly had no interest in stepping out of that circle and becoming the center of attention. What I really wanted at that moment was to be as invisible as possible. But my new bride had other ideas. She was insistent that I had to make even a minor contribution to this family activity. She punctuated her strong feelings with a sharp elbow in my ribs and shoved me out of the circle. This forced me to take a step forward to regain my balance. As all eyes now turned in my direction I quickly reviewed my options. The family hadn't seen me get pushed. I didn't feel that I could step back since to all appearances I had volunteered to retie the chain. I was stuck.

As I walked toward the tractor I thought, "Just calm down. How hard can it be to tie a knot?"

I reached the tractor and picked up the end of the chain which was surprisingly heavy. I wrapped it around the tractor's cross bar several times and tied a big overhand knot. Then I tied another knot and a third just for good measure. I pulled the end of the chain with all of my strength until the huge links cinched as tight against each other as I could get them. I confidently rejoined the circle as the whole group nodded their approval. I had made my contribution, albeit a small one.

A cloud of black diesel smoke belched from the tractor's exhaust pipe as the family patriarch started the iron horse up again. I watched as he put the giant machine in gear and it slowly rolled forward. The slack went out of the chain as it pulled tight against the resisting tree stump. My attention was totally riveted on those knots that I had just so carefully tied. As the tractor inched forward the end of the chain, hanging from the tractor's crossbar, moved up slightly toward the knots. I knew those massive chain links, each was three or four inches long, had to jam tight at any moment.

It's funny how even trivial things can take on enormous importance depending on the circumstances we find ourselves in. At that moment it wasn't fame or riches that I craved. All I wanted most in the entire world was for the knots that I had just tied in that chain to hold fast. As the stump continued to resist the enormous pressure that was placed on it, the end of the chain continued to slowly move.

I thought, "Any second now the chain will have to come to rest as the knots finally cinch up for good."

Beginning to sweat, I watched with growing apprehension as link by enormous link the end of the chain continued to slowly inch up toward the tractor's crossbar. Finally it reached the big ball of knots. I watched in horror as the last knot began to unravel. I just couldn't believe it as the chain slid, like a greased cobra, through each and every one of the knots that I had so carefully tied. The chain finally unwrapped itself from the tractor's crossbar and fell to the ground with a sickeningly loud "CLUNK."

There was a hushed silence as every single member of the assembled family turned in my direction and stared silently at me. No one said a word but they didn't have to. The thought that was clearly on everyone's mind was, "Well, what can you expect from a city boy?"

That was only my second introduction to my wife's family after our wedding. Presently not one of her relatives even seems to remember my embarrassing moment of so many years ago. But to this day, and I've been married a long time, I have not completely forgiven my wife for pushing me out of that circle.

## *Home Away From Home*

When my mother-in-law retired from her teaching job she naturally decided to relocate to the bosom of her family. By that time my wife's great uncle, the family patriarch, had passed away and his house happened to be available. It was a big old place built in 1876 and was just one of many real estate parcels he had purchased in the area during his lifetime. These properties were now held in common by a family corporation.

My mother-in-law bought the house from the family and happily settled in among her relatives. Over the years my wife, our children and I would visit during holidays and special occasions. Ultimately, my mother-in-law passed on and we inherited the house along with the responsibility for its care and upkeep.

After a few years of ownership of the property we were contacted by our insurance company and informed that they needed to double our homeowner's coverage. I threw a fit. I told them that I couldn't sell the house for what they were proposing to insure it for. Double the coverage meant doubling our insurance premiums and I certainly had no interest at all in doing that. The company countered by telling us that if something should happen to the house it could not be replaced because it was currently under-insured. They insisted that if we wanted to continue with their company we had to accept the increased coverage. Although I privately told my wife that I felt this was just a tactic to gouge additional premiums from us, the hapless consumers, we had no choice but to comply.

It was great to be able to have our own place to stay during our visits to Maryland with the family, but since we had retired to Florida, at other times the house stood empty. So when our son told us that he wanted to attend a local Maryland university, it was natural for him to live in our second home surrounded by his cousins.

After a short time he asked if he could invite one of his college friends to be his roommate. We thought this was a great idea as our boy would have company at the house. We had met the friend and knew him to be a responsible young man. So we agreed.

Several months later the family decided to sell off some property. A large building lot was for sale next to the home of one of my wife's cousins and she wanted to know if we were interested in purchasing it.

I asked my wife, "How much land do we need to own in that little town anyway? After all, we have your mother's house."

My bride, always the bargain hunter said, "Listen, it's a very good deal because we will be getting the family price."

To justify any large purchase that she wants to make my wife will often tell me how much we are going to save by buying whatever it is that she wants at a discount. This ploy almost never works on me as I patiently explain that we can save the entire amount by not making the purchase at all. We usually compromise by my giving in for two very good reasons. The first is that I love her. The second is the knowledge that most experienced married men share in common, "If the woman isn't happy, then nobody's happy."

I was still reluctant to spend the money for the extra building lot, but she came up with some other good reasons to convince me. Our old house was on a small parcel some distance from the family. We had talked about the possibility of selling that home and building a new one closer to one of her cousins who lived on a less traveled road. This was an ideal opportunity to acquire just such a building site. If we didn't buy the property it would have to be sold to strangers. Her clincher was to ask, "What if one of our kids wants to build here in the future? We'll have just the spot we need all ready to go." So, partly for the points that she made and partly for the sake of marital peace, we went ahead and bought the extra lot.

## *Fire!*

Another year passed rather uneventfully until one night the phone rang in Florida. The caller was my son who said in a panicky voice, "DAD, THE HOUSE IS ON FIRE!"

No one ever thinks that things like this can happen to him so my immediate reaction was that my son was making a bad joke. "THAT'S NOT FUNNY!"

"I'm not kidding, Dad," he told me. "The house is on fire."

While my son was at work, his roommate decided to make French fried potatoes to accompany his dinner which was cooking on an outdoor grill. He had put some oil in a pan, turned up the heat, and went back outside to check on the barbecue. While he was away the oil reached its flash point and the kitchen was already engulfed when he returned to the house. The roommate called the local volunteer fire department who arrived almost immediately.

As I later learned, old homes like ours can rarely be saved in a house fire. The reason is that these vintage structures were not built with fire breaks to slow the spread of the flames. The lack of fire breaks allows a fire to travel up through the walls unimpeded and the fire then spreads so quickly that all the firemen can usually do is stand by and watch the building burn. Fortunately, the volunteer fire department was located a short distance away and got to our house in minutes. They were soon joined by other fire companies from neighboring communities who cooperated in fighting the blaze. I was told that about fifteen thousand gallons of water were poured on the fire and after a few hours it was extinguished. The house was severely damaged from water and smoke, but still standing. The fireman informed me that most fatalities in a house fire are due to smoke inhalation rather than from the flames themselves. Unfortunately, my son's cat had succumbed to the thick smoke. It was a very good thing that my boy was not at home at the time because he really loved his pet. I'm sure that he would have attempted to rescue his cat with the potential of an even more tragic result.

Living in a small town surrounded by family has many benefits. Close relatives naturally support each other, especially in a time of need. The boys were taken in by one of the cousins until we could figure out what to do next.

I immediately left Florida for Maryland to deal with the aftermath of the fire. My wife was visiting our daughter in New York when she received the startling news. My daughter, seeing that her mother was devastated, dropped everything to drive her hysterical mom down to Maryland. What we found was really depressing. The fire had destroyed the kitchen, porch, family room, two bedrooms and the laundry room, as well as weakened the floor above. Throughout the interior of the house was a layer of soot that covered everything. Mold had already started to grow virtually everywhere because of all the water that had been poured on the building.

After the fire our first meeting with anyone holding an official status was with the Fire Marshal. He told us on the phone that he wanted to interview anyone present when the fire had started and he also needed to verify that the fire was an accident and not arson. After I hung up the phone I thought, "Arson! How can he think that the fire could be arson? Are we under suspicion? Doesn't he understand that people like us don't set fires. Besides, we have an alibi. We were in Florida when the fire broke out." I had to remind myself that he didn't know us and was just doing his job.

Even though I am a scrupulously law abiding person, I get nervous whenever I encounter anyone in law enforcement. I'm not exactly sure why that is. I suppose that since I've gotten my share of traffic tickets that technically makes me a minor law breaker of sorts but I'm still unclear as to why, in the presence of law enforcement types, I get anxious. I suspect most people do.

The Fire Marshal was an older man and, considering his job, had a surprisingly jovial and pleasant manner. As my wife, my son, his roommate and I gathered in the burned out kitchen the Fire Marshal turned to us and said, "Do you want to know how I can tell immediately that this fire was an accident?"

Relieved that we were no longer under suspicion I answered, "Sure."

"You see that the bulb in the kitchen light fixture is completely melted but the one further away in the dining room is only melted on one side. That tells me that no accelerant was used. If the fire had been set it would have moved faster and burned hotter, so both light bulbs would have been completely melted."

The man really knew his job. Then he asked, "How can you tell for sure when a fire has been deliberately started on the Eastern Shore of Maryland?" We looked at him blankly for a moment as he explained. "You can tell that a fire has been set in this area when the only thing that is saved from the blaze is the antique shotgun that had been in the family for generations."

It took us a second before we all realized that he had just made an Eastern Shore arson joke. What we had here was a Fire Marshal with a dark sense of humor. Well, he could afford to joke since he wasn't standing in his own fire ravaged house. He gave us his business card, we shook hands and he went on his way.

## *Well Adjusted*

The next and most important order of business was to meet with the person that essentially held our financial future in his hands; the adjuster from our insurance company. When he arrived, we were impressed with him from our very first meeting. He was a tall broad-shouldered man and carried himself with an almost military bearing. His serious, professional manner made it clear that there would be no jokes about fires coming from this fellow. He told us that he was only sent to cases that were high end losses. Considering that the company had insisted on doubling our home insurance coverage a few years earlier, our loss certainly qualified.

He informed us that unless we decided to hire a Public Adjuster we would be in close contact with him for at least a full year. I asked, "What's a Public Adjuster?" He explained that many times the policy holder opted to hire someone to represent their interests who was not connected to their insurance company. People do this in order to be sure that they will be dealt with fairly. But if we chose to do that all contact between us and the company would immediately cease and all future communications would have to go through the Public Adjuster.

"If you are planning on dealing fairly with us why would I need a Public Adjuster," I suspiciously inquired.

"Of course I'll deal fairly with you, but I'm obligated to inform you of your options."

Although I had a good feeling about this man I knew that, should the need arise at a later date, we could bring in a Public Adjuster. So we opted to stay with the one sent by our insurance company.

After a tour of the fire damaged property the adjuster pronounced the entire structure and its contents a total loss. He explained that extensive smoke damage chemically changes everything that it touches and even hard surfaces like our china dishes could not be salvaged. He told us not to throw anything away as the company would soon be sending someone to inventory the contents of the house. Little did we know what was in store for us.

About two weeks later a man from the inventory company arrived. He was equipped with a clip board, a digital tape recorder, a digital camera and a coal miner's hat that had a light on it. He said that his method of working was to enter a room, pick up the first item and inventory it. He would then throw it over his shoulder, take another step and then inventory the next item before tossing it aside. This was his procedure and he said that he would be in the house for at least a week. He told us that it would be difficult for us to locate things after he was done, so he suggested that we go into the house and retrieve anything that we needed to find before he got started. We did as instructed but there wasn't much that we felt we could salvage.

The inventory man finished his work in six days. One month later we received a large package in the mail. It was an inventory book containing over four thousand lines of our fire damaged possessions. Each line often had multiple items. For example, one had fifty-nine DVDs; another had thirty eight designer tees, another had twenty bath towels; and one line actually had two hundred thirty-eight collector hockey cards. Adding up all the things from every line, there were more like ten thousand items! Everything in the house had been accounted for from the living room sofa to the box of band aids in the medicine chest, and everything had a dollar value.

We had what is known as a full replacement policy on the house and its contents. Most people believe that an insurance company will send the policy holder a check for the full value of a lost item. Wrong! There is a game that all of these companies play and the consumer is often the loser.

The game works like this. Say the item was a table lamp. Our inventory sheet would identify it as follows: One table lamp. Cost: one hundred dollars. Age: six years. Depreciation: fifty percent. Value: fifty dollars. Holdback: twenty five dollars.

Payment: twenty five dollars. Oh yes, even though the item may have been in perfect working order there's depreciation. If the item is not replaced in the time allotted by the company they keep the holdback money. As I said, it's a game and the company usually wins.

So all we would get for our hundred dollar lamp would be twenty five dollars until we replaced it with the same lamp. Only after we submitted our purchase receipt for the new lamp would the company return the twenty five dollars that they held back to us. We would still be out the remaining fifty dollars because of the depreciation. If we went to the store and the same lamp now cost one hundred and fifty dollars we would have to contest the value that the insurance company originally set on the lamp.

The inventory book was easily the size of the average city telephone directory. To deal with just one table lamp was already giving me a headache. The realization that we had over ten thousand items at risk was simply overwhelming. I asked the adjuster how the average working family could possibly find the time and energy to handle the process of replacing their lost property. He said that most people can't and therefore the company often winds up keeping a lot of the holdback money.

Fortunately we were retired at this point and had the time available for all of this. I really should say "she" because my wife embraced the inventory project as if she were on a mission from on high. I'm fortunate to be married to a very organized, detail oriented woman. If it were left to me I would have taken the inventory book and just thrown it away. I simply don't have the head for these kinds of things.

Oh, I did help a little when she asked me to research the value of something on the web. But over a year's time she did what was needed to collect almost what was due us.

Despite all of this aggravation we were still better off than most people who suffer a major loss from a fire. Even though our property was considered a total loss by the insurance company, thankfully most of it was available to be inventoried. Had the house burned to the ground the insurance company would have asked for an itemized list of what was in the building and receipts to prove that we actually had those things.

That would have been an even worse nightmare because we had no idea that we even owned all those thousands of items, and certainly didn't have most of the receipts for them anymore either. Besides, if a house burns to the ground the receipts go up in smoke as well don't they? In that case the company would probably have paid us only a fraction of what they ultimately had to.

The Holdback Game didn't just apply to our lost property. It also applied to the building itself. There was also a full replacement policy on the house. The company informed us that we were obligated to build a home for the full value of the insurance policy or the company would hold back a small fortune. We were faced with a difficult choice. If we built a modest home, which was all we really wanted, the company would keep a significant portion of the value of the policy. If we built to the limit of what we were insured for we would have a home much bigger than we needed, along with higher taxes and maintenance costs. After much deliberation we decided that the insurance company was rich enough and opted to build to the limit of the policy. After all, real estate always goes up in value, doesn't it? At least that's what we thought before the housing bubble burst.

But we weren't finished yet with our fire related problems. We were still the owners of the damaged old house. We had watched as seven dumpsters were filled with the contents of the home and carted away. The building now stood boarded up and empty, while my wife was suffering from feelings of depression and guilt. She felt that somehow she had failed in her duty to be a good custodian of the family home that had been entrusted to her care.

I pointed out to her how irrational those feelings were. Kitchen grease fires are a common occurrence and the fire had been an accident. My logic had little effect as her depression grew. By law we could not just leave the house as it was. We were obligated to either tear it down or rehabilitate it at great expense. We couldn't expect to sell it. Who wants a fire damaged property? I wondered if our problems from the fire were ever going to end.

So what do you do with a fire damaged old house built in 1876? Well, Fate stepped in to answer the question for us. One afternoon we received a call from the head of the local Historical Society. He said that he wanted to meet with us to discuss a business matter. At that meeting we were told that our old house had historical significance. Who knew?

It seems that one of the original founders of the town had built four homes of which ours was the sole surviving example. Over the years the others had all been lost to fires. Even though our house had suffered water and smoke damage, it was essentially intact and the Historical Society wanted to purchase it. Hallelujah! A win, win situation for all of us. It was fortunate that my wife had talked me into buying the extra building lot as it became the ideal site for the new construction.

When I think about the events that led up to the building of our new Maryland house it all seems totally unreal to me. First, the insurance company forced us to double our coverage on the old house. Had they not done that we would not have been able to build the beautiful new home that we did. Then the family decided to sell off some property right where we ultimately wanted to be. I, being the foresighted one, naturally resisted the purchase but fortunately my wife changed my mind. Most importantly, my son wasn't home to attempt a rescue of his cat when the fire started. And finally, the damaged old house turned out to be historically valuable. You know, sometimes it truly is much better to be lucky than smart.

Oh, and our new house: the taxes went way up.

# Ship Ahoy

*Reel Time*

When we moved from Long Island to Florida our grown daughter stayed behind in New York but our teenage son went with us. We had finally realized our dream of an affordable house on the water and he was not about to pass up this opportunity to indulge in his favorite pastime. I had taught my son to fish from an early age and fishing became one of the things that he liked to do best. Our new home was on a canal that led to Charlotte Harbor, a hundred and twenty square mile fisherman's paradise.

Our son planned to attend a Florida university and until his classes began spent as much time as he could fishing. We had not purchased a boat as yet so he contented himself with fishing from the dock. He did pretty well but we knew our waterfront home would not be complete without an accompanying water craft.

Our family was brand new to boating. We had never owned one before and so there were many questions that needed to be answered before such a costly purchase could reasonably be made. The issue of what size, type, and brand of boat continuously occupied our thoughts and conversations.

My wife liked the idea of a boat with a cabin for the comfort and security that style of vessel provided. My son and I preferred a center console fishing boat. My wife felt that a cabin would be the ideal place to put the grandchildren in for their naps when we were all on the water. I pointed out to her that our children were not even engaged as yet so nap time for distant grandchildren should not be a factor in our current decision making. She responded in typical fashion by letting me know that it was never too early to plan for the future.

We went to several boat shows as part of our research. Wandering around one of these nautical extravaganzas I lost track of my wife only to spot her standing on the deck of what appeared to be a small ocean liner. It didn't appear to me, by any stretch of the imagination, to be even remotely affordable for us. Fearing for our financial future I quickly joined her on deck before she rashly signed anything. She was speaking with a hopeful looking salesman as I approached.

Turning to me she said, "Look, darling, this boat has a beautiful complete bathroom and even comes with a lovely pull out sofa." She didn't seem to hear me when I pointed out that we already had a house and were here just to find a boat.

Our interchange was interrupted by the salesman who elaborated, "Folks, with this ship you can go anywhere that you want in complete luxury: The Bahamas, the Caribbean, anywhere."

"Oh," responded my wife, "I don't ever want to leave the harbor."

The salesman's hopeful expression suddenly evaporated never to return. "Excuse me," he said, then turned and presumably went looking for the most recent lottery winner who could at least afford to put gas in the floating hotel we were standing on. It clearly wasn't us.

While our search for the ideal boat continued, my son was spending a lot of time at the local bait and tackle shop. He made friends with several of the old salts there who had definite opinions as to what kind of boat our family should purchase and were not shy about sharing them.

"Listen, kid," they advised, "don't let your folks buy one of those big cabin cruisers. That's what newcomers usually get when they move down here. The wife wants to boat over to Sanibel Island or wherever for lunch. They do this several times and then lose interest. The boat then becomes just an expensive lawn ornament."

The locals told him that Charlotte Harbor is very shallow. Most of the inshore fishing required a smaller boat with a shallow draft so as to fish the "skinny" water where the larger boats couldn't go.

This is the way it went for a while, with no real decision arrived at, until one day my mother called from Fort Lauderdale. She wanted me to supervise the installation of a new bathroom that she needed to put in. So off I went to help Mom out. My son, never one to miss a strategic opportunity, decided to take my wife boat shopping while I was away. I was fully immersed in the bathroom project and up to my hips in grout when I got a call from my wife.

"Listen," she said, "I'm here with your son at a boat store. He's fallen in love with this seventeen foot flats boat which the salesman says is perfect for inshore fishing in the harbor. Is it okay with you if I buy it for him?"

I thought a moment. Our first boat was supposed to be a family affair and I had envisioned something bigger than a seventeen footer. But my wife and I are both pushover parents for our children. Besides, I was dealing with several unexpected plumbing problems for Mom's new bathroom and was not in a mood to think about boats just then. The salesman had also told my wife that the seventeen foot model would be the ideal craft for newcomers to boating, like us, to learn on. The clincher was that it would be much cheaper than any of the larger boats we had considered. So I said, "Get him any darn thing he wants," and returned to the more pressing problems of plumbing Mom's bath. So that's how we got a flats boat instead of a larger vessel.

The salesman turned out to be right. The small boat was indeed perfect for us to practice with. It also turned out to be ideal for banging into the dock, going aground and all the other nautical mistakes that, as inexperienced boaters, we made on a regular basis. These would have been much more traumatic and costly had we purchased a larger more expensive craft.

We were really having a great time with our new purchase. We named it Reel Time. My son was enjoying the boat and happily continued to fill our freezer with finny fillets.

His joy was not complete however, since young men do not live by fish alone. While the boy loved fishing, not surprisingly, he liked girls even better. Unfortunately for him, our area had more retirees for the size of the community than any other place in the country, and accordingly, the dating possibilities for someone his age were pretty slim. He soon made the decision to go to a college in Maryland.

Once he was settled in at his new school, he called frequently to check and make sure that we were taking good care of "his" boat.

"Oh, by the way," he added at the end of each call, "how are you guys doing?" He always was a thoughtful kid.

We used the boat often but found that it was a wet ride. The sides were low and when it was even a little rough out on the harbor we really got drenched. We quickly learned that when the weather turned nasty, we needed to immediately head for home. This was not that big a problem and we generally enjoyed the boat over the next few seasons.

## Ship Mates

Since moving to Florida our circle of friends had not grown very much. Many times I said to my wife that if we wanted to expand our social life we should consider joining something in the community, but we just never seemed to get around to it.

One day we met a nice couple who belonged to a local boat club. They explained that it was not one of those snooty yacht clubs but rather a group of really friendly down-to-earth people sharing a common interest. It was in fact a social club that included boating. They invited us to join. With several hundred members in the club this would be a great opportunity to increase our circle of friends, and to learn more about the harbor and boating in general.

The boat club turned out to be all that was promised and more. The people were warm and welcoming. Everyone seemed to have much more boating experience than we did but were eager to share their knowledge with us newcomers. We quickly made friends with several other couples that had also recently joined. The boat club put out a contact list of all the members which included their phone numbers and the size of the boat they had. In reading the list I observed that we had the dubious distinction of having the smallest vessel in the club. But no matter, we had a boat and so we qualified to belong.

The club offered many different kinds of trips that we could participate in. Since we had a small craft we would be going mostly on the lunch cruises. A few pleasant hours on the water, tie up for lunch at a marina and home again. What could be better? We made several of these trips and really enjoyed them.

The cruises were very well organized. There was a meeting the week before each trip to map out the route to be taken and work out any problems such as weather, location of sand bars, rip currents and the like. At one of these sessions the man who was to be the leader of the forthcoming lunch trip took me aside. "I see that you've signed up for the next cruise," he said.

"That's right," I responded.

"You know that we'll be heading across the harbor for about two hours, don't you?" he continued.

"Yes, I know."

"And will you be taking your seventeen foot boat for the trip?"

Starting to wonder where this was going since we only had the one boat, I said, "Yes, we will. Any problem with that?"

"Oh no, no," he said, "I was just wondering," and he walked away.

What I didn't know at the time was that this man, who was being overly polite, was gently trying to discourage me from taking our small boat on such a long trip across what might be potentially rough water. In retrospect, in light of what later happened, he should just have flat out said, "Stay home!"

The morning of the cruise, as we were getting the boat ready, the flag at the dock began to flap in the breeze. Before joining the club we probably would have gone back into the house to recheck the weather before starting out. But since we had signed up for the lunch trip we felt committed to go. So we simply dismissed this first warning sign and motored out to join up with the others on the harbor.

There were ten boats going on this cruise and all were considerably bigger than ours. When we got to where they were waiting the wind seemed to have increased. Before joining the club this would have been enough for us to immediately head for home and so live to boat another day. But now that we were club members, when the leader signaled that they were ready to leave, instead of wisely turning back, we dumbly followed the group. We didn't want to show poor spirit and we felt, should the need arise, that we had all of these other boats to help us.

The cruise across the harbor was rough for even the larger boats but for us it was terrible. By the time we managed to get our small craft to the marina my wife and I were both soaked to the skin. Oh well, drenched or not we had made it. Now to dry out and enjoy lunch with the group. One of our new friends from the club was along on the trip. We had admired his boat several times and after lunch he gave us a tour. I noticed, with more than a little envy, the flared shape of its hull and the high sides which gave our friend's craft an exceptionally dry ride.

"I saw that you guys had kind of a rough time getting here," he said. "Why don't you follow behind me on the way back and I'll try to flatten the waves out for you as best I can."

"Great idea," I said, noticing that the wind was blowing even harder than it had been earlier.

As we left the shelter of the marina I was horrified to see that conditions had considerably worsened. This day the harbor was clearly no place for a boat of our size to be. The leader of the trip had tried to warn me the week before but I had totally missed it. Nevertheless, there was only one way back home. We had to cross this now very angry body of water.

Our little boat may have been small and light but it was fast. Initially I easily stayed as close behind our friend's larger boat as I safely could. The bigger and more powerful craft did actually manage to flatten the waves out somewhat for us.

The problem was maintaining our speed and holding course. Our boat was taking a pounding as we crashed through the mounting waves breaking over the bow. Once again my wife and I found ourselves instantly drenched. We soon had bigger problems than just wet clothes. Large waves were periodically coming at us from random directions and pushing our bow down. I was forced to cut way back on our speed to prevent our boat from abruptly turning into a submarine. However, by slowing our speed I was falling further behind our friend. With the larger boat no longer flattening out the water for us the growing waves now battered our craft in earnest.

My bride kept exhorting me to catch up with our friend. She was not considering the sea conditions at all and seemed unaware of the serious trouble we were in. In fairness to her she has always had misplaced confidence in her husband. I was terrified, as she should have been, but she thinks that I can handle whatever problem that comes up. In our present circumstances I knew something important and frightening that she didn't. I knew that a positive outcome for this return trip was far from guaranteed.

Whenever I did manage to barely catch up with the larger boat the ferocious wind and random waves forced me to back off. Somehow, and to this day I'm not sure how we did it, we got safely back to the shelter of our own canal.

Our friend, who had kept us in sight just in case, came alongside. His parting words, before he headed for home were, to put it mildly, the understatement of the year. He said with a smile, "I think you guys might need a larger boat."

At the next meeting of the boat club we were approached by many of the members. They had all heard about our horrendous trip and commented on the brave spirit that we had exhibited. They were unaware that on that day bravery had little to do with it. I had been operating purely in survival mode. No one said a word about our lack of intelligence in deciding to go on that trip in the first place. As I said, they were nice people.

## *Reel Time Too*

My wife and I quickly decided that if we were to remain members of the club a larger boat was absolutely necessary. We justified the expense in two ways. We had a major wedding anniversary coming up and a bigger boat would be an ideal gift to give to each other. The second reason was that we now considered a larger craft to be nothing short of life insurance.

We dragged out the piles of brochures that we had amassed from all of the boat shows that we had gone to and reexamined the features of each and every one. Then, out of the blue, my wife suggested that we consider getting the same boat that our friend had, the one that we had tried to follow across the harbor.

"That boat is way too expensive for us," I told her. "I remembered seeing it at one of the shows a few years before. Price-wise it had been way out of our league."

"It was just an idea," she said. "I really liked that one but if it's too expensive just forget it."

I also loved our friend's boat but I felt there was no way we could afford it. But over the next few days I couldn't help thinking that maybe my wife had been right, just maybe we could swing it. Why not get a used boat? After all, the economy was way down and there were no doubt many bargains to be had. I was searching the web when I came upon an ad for the identical boat that our friend had. This was a brand new leftover model. The ad said, "Price too low to quote here. Please call."

I couldn't dial the phone fast enough. When I connected with a salesman I was amazed to find that the cost for this new leftover model was far cheaper than lesser quality boats had been selling for just a few years earlier. In addition, the manufacturer was offering a tremendous rebate to get rid of their last year's models.

The boat came fully equipped with quality electronics and many accessories. The dealer was located over a hundred miles away but the salesman said that he would wave the normal thousand dollar delivery charge and transport the boat to us for free. This deal was just too good to pass up. My wife and I decided to go for it.

A week later a large truck pulling an even larger trailer showed up at our house. Our new boat had arrived and boy, was it ever a beauty. The driver launched it at a local ramp and gave us a test ride. It ran like a top and the ride was bone dry. We were thrilled and decided to name this one Reel Time Too.

We took the boat out a few times and loved every minute of it. The new engine was not even broken in yet when we reluctantly had to abandon our new toy and travel up north. It was holiday time and we needed to be with the family. A short visit turned into a six week stay. I couldn't wait to leave the cold weather and get back to Florida.

## *I Smell a Rat*

The morning after we returned home from Maryland I hurried outside to check on the boat. There she sat, gleaming in the sun and even more beautiful than I remembered. As I stood there on the dock I was really feeling the pride of ownership of our new purchase. That I would ever get to own such a prestigious craft had been an impossible dream just a few years earlier. I got on board and opened the door to the center console where I kept most of our equipment. The boat had come from the dealer with a complete Coast Guard Package. Most of the new life jackets were still in their plastic bags and I wanted to unwrap them.

There was something not right about the first one I picked up. The plastic had a hole in it. And what was this? The paper label inside was shredded as if something had chewed it. Examining it more closely I could see that something had indeed been chomping away. It was then that I noticed what looked like large grains of black rice scattered around on the floor of the center console. Where had all this black rice come from? I thought rice was white.

Then it hit me. "It isn't rice at all, it's poop! Rat poop! Yuck! We have RATS!" There were rats on my beautiful new boat. I was totally freaked out.

I was sure that I had locked the door to the center console before we left for our trip. So how had the little buggers gotten into this locked compartment? A search revealed a large drain hole in the floor. This was to allow any water that might get in to drain down into the bilge below. So that's where they are. They're under the floor. Somehow they got on board, managed to get below and came up into the locked storage area. I hurried back on deck to locate the entry points where they had gained access.

Every boat manufacturer has different design features for their products. Our boat had several holes in the top of each railing that served as fishing rod holders. Unfortunately they connected directly to the bilge below the floor of the boat. I noted that these small holes might be the possible points of entry for our furry invaders. Next I noticed two large vent ports near the stern seat. They were there to allow any gas fumes that might build up below the deck to safely escape from the bilge. But these holes were much bigger than the rod holders. A cheetah could have easily gotten through them! I decided that this was where the dirty little rats probably got in.

I went back to the house to break the disturbing news to my bride.

She called to me as I entered the kitchen, "So, how's the boat?"

"Not so good. We have stowaways."

She gave me a blank look and asked, "What do you mean stowaways?"

"I mean we have rats on board."

"Rats! How can we have rats?" she demanded to know. "We've lived here for years and have never seen a rat!"

She does this to me all the time. It's as if she believes that her demanding question will instantly make the problem disappear. I patiently explained to her all that I had discovered in the last few traumatic minutes.

"Well, we certainly can't have rats on the boat," she declared, as if giving me new information. "What are 'We' going to do about it?" The use of 'We', as any married man will immediately recognize, meant 'Me'.

I patiently explained, "First, 'We' are going to get rid of the rats that are on board and then we're going to prevent their friends from coming back."

By way of encouragement she demanded, "Well then, you'd better hurry up and do that. And don't tell any of the neighbors that we have rats!"

So off I went to find a solution to our problem rodentia.

"I have rats," I announced to the man in the hardware store.

"You mean you have rats in your house?"

"Oh, no, they're on my new boat. How do I get rid of them?"

He told me, "Rats are smart critters and are not so easy to get rid of. There are two ways to go. One way is poison. Once a rat eats the poisoned bait it'll takes three or four days to kill lt. The problem is if the rats die in a location where you can't remove them they can stink up the place." The idea of a dead rat stuck way up under the deck and smelling up my boat was not appealing in the least.

"What's the other way?"

"Traps. That's what I would do if I were you. The glue traps work well," he offered.

Being brand new to the problem I asked, "What's a glue trap?"

He explained that it was a heavy piece of cardboard coated with a super sticky flavored glue. "When the rat gets stuck on it you can wait until it dies or you can dispatch it yourself."

Not only am I basically a pacifist but I'm a squeamish one as well. The thought of an unfortunate critter, even a lowly rat, stuck on a glue trap waiting for me to finish it off was not something that I thought I could easily deal with.

"What else do you have?"

"Well, there are live traps. You catch the rats alive and you then can decide what to do with them."

Still in unfamiliar territory I naively asked, "What does one do with trapped rats?"

"Well, some people drive them a distance away and release them but most just sink the cage in water and drown them."

This did not sound to me like a terrific approach either. I didn't think that driving my rats around town and releasing them to infest other people's houses and boats would make me very popular in the community. Also, watching a hapless creature gasping for air until it drowned was not something I thought I could comfortably handle.

"Anything else?" I asked.

"A lot of people use the snap traps." The man showed me how to pull back and set the heavy spring which, when triggered by the rodent, would instantly send it to Rat Heaven.

I decided that this was the best of a bad lot. At least the end would come quickly for Minnie or Mickey and they wouldn't suffer. I could set the snap traps and not have to be present at the execution.

I returned home, baited several of the traps with peanut butter and distributed them liberally on the boat. Then I went back into the house to wait for results.

I informed my bride that her mighty hunter was now fully on the job and our rat problem would soon be a thing of the past.

"How come we never had rats on the little boat?" she asked. She always expects me to have an immediate and accurate answer to just about any question she asks.

The best one I could come up on the spur of the moment was, "Well, maybe these are upper class rats and will only board the larger more expensive vessels."

Not at all amused by my response she gave me her famous "you'll pay for that later" look and walked away.

That night our dog was furiously barking at the front door and I went out to see what was going on. A car was on the street in front of our house pulling forward and backing up and then repeating the process over and over again. I approached the car to investigate this very strange behavior. The driver was one of our neighbors who lived further down the street. When I asked her what she was doing she told me that she had just run over a rat in the road. I looked toward the front of her car and saw, illuminated by the headlights, what looked like a rat shaped pancake.

Not content with merely killing the poor thing my neighbor had felt the need to run over it multiple times. She explained that they had rats on their very expensive cabin cruiser. The rodents had chewed most of the wires on their boat and caused at least ten thousand dollars worth of damage. Since she hated these critters so much this was her small revenge. Apparently, not only did our neighbors already know about the rats in our neighborhood, they already had some of their own!

"I didn't know that you had rats," I impolitely observed.

"We live on the water. Everyone in this development has tree rats."

This was a new animal for me. Back in New York City there were giant sewer rats that even the battle-hardened alley cats were afraid of. I had never heard of tree rats before so I asked my neighbor to elaborate. She told me that our Florida rats often inhabited the Palm trees, hence the name. They were smaller than their New York cousins but were just as prolific and destructive. After this short rat tutorial she asked, "Don't you have them too?"

"Well, uh, yes," I said weakly, "I do now."

"Well then, good luck," she said and with that she rolled over the rat pancake one more time and drove away.

I went back inside to share the news with my wife that we had built our house smack in the middle of Rat Central.

"Since everyone here seems to have them, why hasn't anyone said a word about rats to us before now?" I asked her.

"It's simple. No one wants to admit that they have vermin on their property. It's just not the kind of thing you'd want to publicize."

Well I didn't feel that way at all. Now that the rat was out of the bag, so to speak, I began to interview our neighbors to see how they were handling their own rat problems and gather as many tips on rat control as I could. One fellow, who also had a large cabin cruiser, had put his cat on the boat for a week. His furry stowaways promptly left never to return. He explained that rats will not live or nest anywhere there are predators around.

We had two cats of our own but our boat was not as large as his. Besides, our cats were used to the good life indoors and would probably freak out if I put them on the boat.

In the meanwhile I decided to check my traps which by now had been standing guard for a couple of days. I remembered to bring along a garbage bag to dispose of the rodent remains. I soon returned to the house totally dejected.

"Well, how'd you do?"

I told her, "The score so far is rats one, boat owner zero."

"Explain, please."

"There is rat poop all over the deck and down in the center console of the boat. Some of the traps have been sprung and the peanut butter bait eaten. Some traps are not sprung but the bait is also gone."

"You didn't catch any?" she admonished.

I shook the empty garbage bag for emphasis and slumped down in a chair. "Not one. This is going to be a bigger problem than I thought. We just might have the Albert Einsteins of the rat world on our boat," I informed her.

"Then maybe we should get professional help," she offered. My thoughts went to my neighbor with the expensive wiring damage. The idea of these dirty little monsters busily chewing away on our brand new boat was horrifying to me, so I grabbed the phone book and dialed an exterminator. I became even more horrified when he told me that he wanted one hundred and twenty five dollars for his first visit and sixty five dollars for each additional trip. He couldn't tell me how many of these trips might be necessary because rat control was such a difficult problem. He also said that there were no guarantees.

This all sounded much too expensive. When I told him that my neighbor had gotten rid of his rats for the price of a couple of cans of cat food with just the aid of the family pet, he responded, "Your neighbor got lucky." I told the exterminator that I would have to think about his service and hung up.

The only thing that I knew for sure at this point was that I was dealing with tree rats and that a cat could get rid of them. My traps weren't working. As I often do, I turned to my computer for an answer. Once on the Web I typed in, "Controlling Tree Rats" and, to my surprise, several hundred pages on the subject popped up.

The first disturbing fact that I discovered was that one amorous tree rat couple, if left undisturbed for just a single year, would result in an unbelievable rodent population of over fifteen thousand progeny. At that rate of reproduction I feared my new boat would be chewed right down to the water line.

In a near panic, I searched the various web sites for a solution. One particular site caught my eye. "Rid your home or boat of rats the humane way," proclaimed the advertisement. This company was selling what they described as a glandular extract that was taken from bobcats and foxes. I forced myself to try and not picture how they went about acquiring such a product. Their miracle repellent, as they called it, came in granular form. The idea was to sprinkle some of this stuff around where it was needed and the rats would decide that a sudden population explosion of their natural predators had just moved in. The rats would then promptly abandon ship.

"Wow," I thought, "this is just like what my neighbor had done with his cat. It has to work!"

I called the company and ordered their largest package of repellent and even paid extra for overnight shipping.

"I'll show that exterminator I don't need him," I thought.

When the bobcat and fox repellent arrived I wasted no time in distributing the granules liberally around the boat. In the process I noticed that our resident rodents had blissfully continued consuming the bait from my traps without managing to spring even a single one. Oh well, no matter, now that I had both bobcats and foxes on my team I was sure our problem would soon be solved.

I told my bride that she could now relax and that all would be well.

"Assuming this fox stuff actually works, how will you know when or if the rodents have left the boat?" she asked. She hadn't dared to go on board since I discovered our furry invaders and hadn't seen what I had.

"Listen," I reassured her, "the only thing that a rat does as well as making little rats, is poop. The stuff is all over the boat. Every time that I clean it up the next day there's more to deal with. We'll know that our furry friends are gone when they take their poop with them. No more rat droppings means there are no more rats."

"All right. I just hope this works."

"Of course it'll work. The company guarantees it."

The literature that came with the repellant said that it might take a few days for it to do its job. But a week later when I had to buy a second jar of peanut butter to bait the traps I was forced to admit that the bobcat and fox repellent was a complete and total failure. I suppose that since we hadn't gotten any bobcats or foxes on the boat it must have effectively repelled those critters but it sure didn't work on rodents.

Now, more than a little crazed, I stood on the deck of our new boat and announced to all those in residence below. "O.K., listen up you rats. You may have beaten me but I'm now going to get professional help. Your days are numbered! You hear me?" As I said, I was a little crazed.

The exterminator arrived in an unmarked van. He wore an official looking uniform and wore white cotton gloves. He said that most people in need of his services didn't want to advertise that fact and so his vehicle had no identification on it.

I decided not to point out that this effort at discretion was not very well supported by his uniform since the name of the extermination company was prominently emblazoned on the back of his shirt. Instead, I told him that for all I cared he could put a neon sign up on my roof if he wanted to as long as he solved our rat problem.

He promised, "I'll do my best."

After checking out my boat and the dock area, he announced, "I recommend that you organize your neighbors and let our company treat the entire waterfront along your development on a regular basis. What you have here is prime tree rat habitat. Without controlling the whole population of rodents, I can't guarantee you anything."

This was not exactly the news I expected to hear. I'm really not a very organized person. In fact, I'm someone who even has trouble neatly arranging my sock drawer. I certainly didn't feel up to the task of organizing the entire development. Besides, it suddenly appeared to me as if this exterminator was not so much interested in a job but was really after a lifetime annuity.

"Why don't we just start with my place and I'll see about talking to my neighbors later."

Obviously concerned that his annuity might be in jeopardy he craftily replied, "All right, but without treating the whole neighborhood, as I told you, there are no guarantees."

I said that my snap traps were not working. He asked if I had worn gloves when I sent the traps.

"Why did I need gloves?" I wondered.

He told me that a tree rat is one very canny critter. "The human scent makes them extra cautious." I had no idea that smelly rats were so particular. He removed my snap traps and replaced them with his own. Now I understood his white cotton gloves.

He then informed me that if a rat sees another of its kind caught in a trap those traps will no longer work. In other words, the little buggers were really quick learners. The exterminator also put out several closed boxes that had rat sized holes cut in their sides. Inside the boxes he placed poisoned bait that he told me the rats would find irresistible. He insisted that only licensed professional exterminators could get this bait or these special bait boxes. He said that he would be back to check on things the following week and left.

Later I ran into the neighbor who had suffered all that wiring damage on his big cabin cruiser. I shared with him what we had been going through and how I had been forced to call the exterminator.

"Didn't you once tell me that you were a pacifist?" he asked.

"I am," I responded. "You've heard the expression that there are no atheists in fox holes? Well let me tell you, there are no pacifists in rat holes either. Especially when the rats are on my boat."

"Well, good luck. But I'm getting rid of my cabin cruiser."

"Why? Are you still dealing with a rat problem?"

"I wish. Just yesterday I went on board, opened the cabin door and you know what I found? There were three raccoons lounging on the bunk. They weren't even the least concerned and looked at me with a 'Yeah, and what do you want?' attitude. I'm totally fed up. So I called a broker and told him to come and just take the boat away. I don't even care any more what I get for it."

"Did you call animal control for the raccoons?"

"Nah, the boat dealer can have them too. I'm done."

Listening to my neighbor's story was truly disturbing. First rats, then raccoons. "What's next," I wondered, "mountain lions?"

I told my wife that I couldn't understand why the manufacturer of our boat had incorporated so many potential rat holes into our boat's design. Always the one to look on the bright side she said, "Maybe it's because most of the boats that they sell are not delivered to rat infested neighborhoods."

Everyone needs a shoulder to cry on so by now I had shared the news of our rodent problem with anyone who would listen. I was shocked at how many people knew all about tree rats in our community.

At about this time my wife decided to host a birthday party for me. My friends arrived with interesting presents. A beautifully gift wrapped package of cheese was an especially thoughtful one. I was also presented with mouse and rat traps of various kinds. But my favorite gift of all was a Pied Piper hat and a flute. So now, besides having a rat problem, I was to be the butt of jokes in our social circle.

The rat humor I could deal with, the actual rats were another thing entirely. I was consumed with worry. The exterminator's foolproof bait wasn't working and neither were his traps. At the point when I was totally at my wits end, just like that, our furry stowaways were suddenly gone. We were sure they had left because they were thoughtful enough to take their black rice with them. No more rat poop meant no more rats. But why had the little buggers headed for the hills? I later found the answer. All of the turmoil that I had gone through ultimately turned out to be unnecessary. Rats are similar to people in a lot of ways. They just don't like being disturbed. They had moved in on our boat because we had been away for so long. Now that we were back and I was paying regular visits to the boat again, the rats decided to abandon ship. I just hoped that wasn't their way of commenting on my questionable seamanship.

A friend helped me close up the vent holes with wire mesh and I put rubber stoppers in all the rod holders. This prevented any chance our rats, or any of their friends, could ever gain entrance again. Reel Time Too was now a totally rat free zone. When I broke the news to the exterminator that we no longer required his services his cynical response was, "We'll see."

By some miracle our boat had been spared any wiring or other damage. This I decided must have been because I had thoughtfully supplied our furry stowaways with an endless supply of peanut butter so there was no need for them to chew on anything else. There was collateral damage however. By the end of this torturous rat race my nerves were totally shot.

I suppose what I took away from all this was that, ultimately, we were really fortunate. If we had bought a cabin cruiser like my bride originally wanted, by now we'd probably have a serious raccoon problem!

## *Epilogue:*
## The Pelican Incident

The expectations of confirmed pessimists are usually negative. However, if the sky does not fall at the expected time, committed pessimists paradoxically may have mixed feelings. On the one hand, since the anticipated calamity did not occur, there is a natural sense of relief. On the other, they may not be able to suppress a feeling of unease since their unfulfilled expectation conflicts with their negative viewpoint. Today might have turned out O.K., but the entrenched pessimist remains convinced that tomorrow is definitely going to be worse.

I once knew a very pessimistic woman who, upon being told something as innocuous as, "It's a beautiful day," gazed up at a bright, clear blue sky and declared, "It looks like it's probably going to rain tomorrow." A person this invested in a negative outlook on life is closing herself off from positive experiences and relationships with other people. Unfortunately, since pessimists generally expect the worst to happen, they often unknowingly trigger a chain of events designed to create a self-fulfilling prophesy and sabotage themselves.

If calmly accepting your unfulfilled expectations doesn't sit too well with all of you die-hard pessimists, then I'd like to share a final experience that has helped to modify my own pessimistic thinking.

There is a married couple that my wife and I have become very good friends with in recent years. They are always fun to be around because they are committed to enjoying life more than just about any other people that we know. When they encounter negative individuals or negative situations they do their best to avoid getting involved with either. They are the prototypical people who, if life gives them lemons they try and make darn sure that they at least get some lemonade.

Our friends rent a house during the winter months near where we live on the west coast of Florida. They are avid fisher folk and are both very good at it. One day I read in the paper that the sheepshead were coming into near shore waters. These fish were reported to be very good eating but I had never caught one. My buddy offered to take me to a pier where he knew that we were sure to meet with success.

A few days later my wife and I threw our fishing tackle into the car and off we went to join our friends. When we got to the pier we all walked out to the end because that was supposed to be the best spot for sheepshead. The four of us had arrived early enough so we were the only occupants of the pier, with the exception of a half dozen hopeful pelicans that stood by patiently looking for a handout.

After setting up the fishing rods, sure enough, my friend caught the first fish. He usually does, as he is really an expert fisherman. He then proceeded to catch numbers two and three as well. On the other hand my wife and I were getting bites but no fish. Sheepshead are notorious bait stealers and you have to set the hook almost before you feel a nibble. I wasn't sure that I would eventually get one but in the mean time I was having a lot of fun trying. As I was attempting to outwit the wily sheepshead, two other fishermen arrived on the pier and stopped near where we were fishing. Not doing too well with us, the resident panhandling pelicans turned their attention to these two newcomers.

One of the men removed a bait fish from a bucket and hooked it about three feet under a large float. As he cast out from the pier, one of the pelicans, seeing an opportunity for a free meal, flew down and landed near the man's bait.

Any reasonably intelligent fisherman would have pulled the bait quickly away from the feathery felon and reeled in as fast as possible to avoid hooking the bird. Unfortunately, this fisherman was neither reasonable nor intelligent. As the pelican pursued what he thought was a free meal this unsportsmanlike boob made only a half hearted attempt to move the bait away. The pelican continued its pursuit as the man weakly jerked his line again, but this time he succeeded in hooking the hapless bird.

Now, a responsible person who found themselves with a pelican on the other end of his fishing line would make every effort to gently bring it in and carefully unhook the poor creature. Not this bozo. Instead, he took a few turns on his reel, then muttering some curses took out a pocket knife and cut the line. The hapless pelican flew over the pier trailing the large float and a long length of the fishing line from its beak.

I was livid. I couldn't believe this idiot fisherman could have been so callous. His actions had condemned the unfortunate bird to a slow and torturous demise. I voiced my anger to our friends as I was deciding whether to confront the guy.

My buddy, who was unhooking yet another sheepshead, turned to me and casually asked, "Are we going to have a good day or not?"

Knowing my friend as I did it suddenly hit me that this wasn't just an idle question. It was actually advice. I realized that his simple inquiry really contained within it multiple meanings. I mentally reviewed them, one by one. The pelican had flown away and I couldn't help him. Confronting the jerk that hooked it will not transform the man into any less of a jerk. If my confrontation results in a physical altercation, then one or both of us could be hurt and still nothing would change for the bird. I also might even end up with a legal problem. So, in my righteous anger, all I could do is create further problems and upset for myself and everyone around me. Or, I could chose to have a good day despite what had just happened.

Choice is the important point to be made here. Suddenly, standing on that pier, I had the revelation that I had the power to choose. Understanding that although I could not change the upsetting events that had just occurred, or the person responsible, I could change my response to what I had witnessed. I could choose to have a good day anyway. Why had I not come to this understanding years before? Thinking about it, I probably did; but somewhere along the way I had lost this important concept. Now that I had it back I grasped it tightly as an emotional life preserver.

The larger message which I still try to follow is that all of us can choose to have "A Good Day" most of the time. Instead, we let outside events, as I almost did on that pier, dictate the kind of day or week, or month, or year, or by extension even the kind of life we will ultimately lead. So now when I turn on the morning news and none of it is good I choose to turn it off and have a pleasant day anyway. I call this the "power of the pelican incident".

My wish for you is that you will operate from choice. Decide that each and every day will be a good one and your glass should always remain half full.

www.ingramcontent.com/pod-product-compliance
Lightning Source LLC
Chambersburg PA
CBHW071652090426
42738CB00009B/1500